FROM BAGHDAD, WITH LOVE

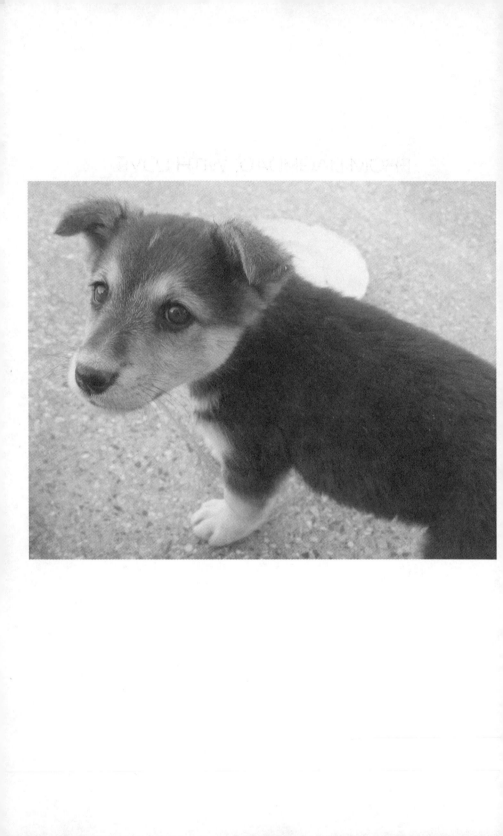

FROM BAGHDAD, WITH LOVE

A DOG, A MARINE, AND THE LOVE THAT SAVED THEM

UPDATED EDITION

LTCOL JAY KOPELMAN

with MELINDA ROTH and TOM MCCARTHY

LYONS
PRESS

Guilford, Connecticut

An imprint of The Rowman & Littlefield Publishing Group, Inc.
4501 Forbes Blvd., Ste. 200
Lanham, MD 20706
www.rowman.com

Distributed by NATIONAL BOOK NETWORK

British Library Cataloguing in Publication Information available

Library of Congress Cataloging-in-Publication Data available

ISBN 978-1-4930-4206-7 (paperback)
ISBN 978-1-4930-4207-4 (e-book)

♾™ The paper used in this publication meets the minimum requirements of American
National Standard for Information Sciences—Permanence of Paper for Printed Library
Materials, ANSI/NISO Z39.48-1992.

To Lava

INTRODUCTION TO THE NEW EDITION

MY TIME IN Fallujah is distant now and purposefully so. I could put myself back there in an instant if I chose to. A lot of things can still send me back there—a loud, sudden noise, a certain smell, a call from another Marine, like Tim O'Brien, who came for a visit last September. I've worked hard to guard against those sudden and unwelcome intrusions in my life these days. I prefer not to look back on those crazy, chaotic time. Look back but don't stare, they say about dark memories. Take whatever they gave you, but don't dwell on them or stand too close to the edge lest you fall into the crevasse.

When it comes to thinking about Fallujah I do make one exception to that rule. Lava.

I can still smile when I think about meeting Lava and what he did for me in Fallujah—what he did for so many of us Marines and for the people who fell in love with him.

I never bury those days.

You'll understand the reason why soon enough.

First week of the US invasion of Fallujah, Iraq

IN AN ABANDONED house in the northeast section of Fallujah, members of the First Battalion, Third Marines—known as the Lava Dogs—froze when they heard a series of clicks coming from the one remaining room of the compound.

Grenade pins?

Most of the military deaths in Fallujah during that first week of the US invasion happened inside buildings like this, where insurgents hid in upper rooms and threw grenades down at the Marines as they moved upward. There were a lot of head and face injuries, and while the Lava Dogs considered themselves some of the toughest Marines around—they named themselves out of respect for the jagged pumice they trained on back in Hawaii—just being a Lava Dog didn't shield you from a grenade's fancy special effects. Being careful did. Being focused did. Having your weapon locked and loaded when you inched around every corner did.

Click. Click. Click . . . Click.

If a grenade did detach your face from your skull, at least you would check out in the GPS coordinate closest to Heaven. Iraq was considered by most biblical archaeologists to be the location of the

Garden of Eden—God's only hard copy of Heaven, his Paradise on earth. Not that you'd have adequate excuses prepared once you got there, because lines between good and evil here in the battle zone required more than reading glasses to see. But whether Abraham, Muhammad, or Jesus called your cadence, it's where it officially all started and where it officially all went bad.

Good marketing potential for the region at first, though, because it trademarked the birthplace of Abraham, the Tower of Babel, and the construction of Babylon in addition to agriculture, writing, the wheel, the zodiac, legal theory, bureaucracy, and urbanization. From the beginning, everyone wanted a piece of the place that went from the Mesopotamians to the Sumerians to the Akkadians to the Empire of Ur to the Babylonians to the Assyrians to the Persians to the Greeks to the Arabs to the Mongols to the Turks to the British.

None of these were polite handovers, either. By the time Saddam Hussein got to the land of milk and honey, it had been captured, pillaged, beaten, and raped by so many cultures over such a long period of time, there was little left except a whole lot of desert covering a whole lot of oil. That, and claims by locals living near the Tigris and Euphrates Rivers that the Garden of Eden and its Tree of Life stood in the middle of their very town. They built a wall around the area, constructed the Garden of Eden Hotel, and tourism flourished for a short while. Then the Americans came, and because the folks living in the area supported the newest invasion, Hussein drained all their water. Soon the Tree of Life died, members of the Supreme Council for the Islamic Revolution in Iraq took over the Garden of Eden Hotel, and DOWN WITH AMERICANS was painted all over the walls of Paradise.

Clickclickclickclick.

Maybe timed explosives.

If this country was Paradise, then the Marines weren't taking any bets on Hell. Outside the building they searched, gunships prowled the skies looking for hiding insurgents as pockmarked Humvees patrolled what was left of the streets. Every driving car in the city was targeted because of bomb risks. Every loose wire was suspect. Every building was searched, and JIHAD, JIHAD, JIHAD plastered every wall.

Throughout the first days of the invasion of Fallujah, the Marines discovered weapons caches, suicide vests, and large amounts of heroin, speed, and cocaine apparently used to bolster suicide bombers' courage. They found dead bodies of fighters from Chechnya, Syria, Libya, Jordan, Afghanistan, and Saudi Arabia. They walked into human slaughterhouses with hooks hanging from the ceilings, black masks, knives, bloody straw mats, and videos of beheadings. They freed emaciated prisoners shackled and insane with fear.

Fallujah, near the center of where it all began, was now a city cordoned off from the rest of the world, inhabited only by invisible snipers and stray dogs feasting on the dead.

Click. Snuffle. Snuffle. Click.

The Lava Dogs tightened their jaws and clenched their weapons as they ran through the rules in their heads: Cover danger areas, stay low, move stealthily, be prepared to adapt, and eliminate threats.

Snuffle. Clickclickclick. Snufflesnuffle.

An insurgent strapping a bomb to his chest?

They should have prepped the room first with a grenade—tossed it in and just let it do all the dirty work. Instead, for reasons still obscured by war and fear and things just destined to be, they backed up to the walls on either side of the doorway and positioned their weapons to fire.

Then they thrust their rifles around the corner, squared off, and zeroed in on the clicks as their target rushed to the other side of the room.

"Holy shit."

The puppy turned at the sound of their voices and stared at them.

"What the hell?"

He cocked his head, trying to interpret their intent rather than their words.

"You gotta be kidding."

Then he yipped, wagged his tail, and clicked his toenails on the floor as he pranced up and down in place, happy it seemed someone had found him at last.

PART I

"In toil you shall eat of it all the days of your life."

Genesis 3:17

CHAPTER ONE

November 2004
Fallujah

I DON'T REMEMBER exactly when I got to the house that served as our command post in the northwest sector of Fallujah, and I don't remember exactly how I got there. It was a couple of days after the Lava Dogs arrived and took over the compound, I do know that much, and I remember that after four days of dodging sniper fire, sleeping on the ground, and patrolling Fallujah with wide-eyed Iraqi soldiers in training who shot at anything that moved, including their own boots, I walked up to the building with a sense of having escaped an abstract rendition of the wrong hereafter.

I remember being exhausted, the tiredness weighing more heavily on me than the sixty-pound rucksack I lugged around, and as I walked through the front door and shrugged what I could off my back, all I could think about was sleep.

That's when I saw Lava for the first time. Only it's not as if I walked in and saw a chubby puppy cuddled up on a blanket undefiled by the world like an overstuffed lamb. There were no squeaky toys, no baby yips, no eyes looking up at me with an artless blue-gray innocence.

Instead a sudden flash of something rolls toward me out of no-where, shooting so much adrenaline into my wiring that I jump back and slam into a wall. A ball of fur not much bigger than a grenade skids across the floor, screeches to a halt at my boots, and then whirls in circles around me with the torque of a windup toy. It scares me, right? Like I'm tired and wired and anything quick coming at me jerked at my nerves, so I peel back off the wall and reach for my rifle even though I can see it's only a puppy.

Now, before you get all out of whack about me aiming a weapon at cute baby mammals, keep in mind that I just walked in from the streets. Out there, things were spooky, like a plague or a flood or dust from an atomic bomb had just rolled through. Most of the city fled before the US-led attack, and the quiet rang so loud after the bombardment, even windblown newspaper sent your nerves screaming for solid cover.

The day before the offensive started, we dropped leaflets over the city warning the few remaining citizens that we were on our way in, but insurgents inside spit back that they had hundreds of car bombs rigged, booby traps set, and suicide bombers with jittery fingers waiting to go. They'd already dug trenches in the city's cemeteries for the expected martyrs.

In the days prior to our march into the city, our warplanes pounded Fallujah with cannon fire, rockets, and bombs. Because the skies were so crowded, attack jets had only a three-minute window to unload their cargo and clear out before another jet swooped in. Hundreds and hundreds of pounds of 105mm shells, 25mm rounds, and 40mm rounds blasted into Fallujah that night with the impact of meteors from several galaxies away. The aerial bombardment was so spectacular, I—along with ten thousand other Marines waiting to advance on the outskirts of the city—doubted anyone inside would live through it. But plenty managed, and now that we were here, sniper fire came at us from nowhere like the screams from ghosts.

So when this unexpected thing, this puppy, comes barreling toward me in this unexpected place, I reach for my gun. I must have yelled or something, because at the sound of my voice, the puppy looks up at me, raises his tail, and starts growling this baby-dog version of *I am about to kick your ass*.

The fur gets all puffy around his neck like he's trying to make himself look big, and then he lets loose these wienie war cries—*roo-roo-roo-rooo*—as he bounces up and down on stiff legs.

I stomp my boot his way to quiet him down, but he doesn't budge and intensifies the *roo-roo-roo-roooos* shooting in staccato from his lungs.

"Hey."

I shove the rifle to my back and bend down. The puppy bounces backward in time to the *roo-roo-roo-roooos* but doesn't take his eyes from my face.

"Hey. Calm down."

He looks like a bloated panda bear, and when he howls the last *rooooo* of the *roo-roo-rooooo*, his snout stretches skyward until his fat front paws lift off the floor.

There's fear in his eyes despite the bravado. He's only a puppy, too young to know how to mask it, so I can see how bravery and terror trap him on all sides while testosterone and adrenaline compete in the meantime for every ounce of his attention. Recognize it right away.

I reach into my pocket, *roo-roo-roo*, pull out a bullet, *roo-roo-roo-roo*, and hold it out toward him in hopes he'll think it's food. The puppy stops barking and cocks his head, which makes me feel manipulative but wise.

"Thatta boy."

He sniffs the air above his head, finds nothing, and then directs his nose toward the bullet. It interests him, and he leans forward for a better whiff of the metal, which surprises me until I notice how filthy my hands are, almost black from a week without washing, and I realize he's smelling accumulated dirt and death on my skin.

I lean forward, but fear gets the better of him and he tears off down the hall.

"Hey, come back."

I stand there and watch him career into a wall. I wince, that's got to hurt, but he gets up, shakes his head, and takes off again.

"Hey, come here."

The puppy stops and looks back at me, ears high, tiny tail rotating wildly, pink tongue hanging out sideways from his mouth like he's crazy. I realize he wants me to chase him, like he figured out he was bamboozled only he's too proud to admit it and now covers up with this *I-was-never-afraid-of-you* routine. I recognize that one, too.

He leaps in a circle on paws as big as his face, hits the wall again, and repels into a puddle of daze. I'm, like, mesmerized by the little guy. Wipes my windshield clean just watching him, so I scoop him up off the ground with one hand and pretend I didn't notice his wall slam.

"Tough guy, huh?"

He smells like kerosene.

"What's that aftershave you're wearing?"

He feels lighter than a pint of bottled water as he squirms and laps at my face, blackened from explosive residue, soot from bombed-out buildings, and dust from hitting the ground so many times.

"Where'd you come from?"

I have a pretty good idea where he came from and a pretty good idea where he's going, too. I've seen it before, Marines letting their guards down and getting too friendly with the locals—pretty girls, little kids, cute furry mammals, doesn't matter; it's not allowed. So as I'm holding the little tough guy and he's acting like he just jumped out of a box under the Christmas tree, I call my cool to attention.

It's not allowed, Kopelman.

But he keeps licking and squirming and wiggling around, and I remember this part pretty well, because I liked the way he felt in my hands, I liked that he forgave me for scaring him, I liked not caring about getting home or staying alive or feeling warped as a human being—just him wiggling around in my hands, wiping all the grime off my face.

CHAPTER TWO

November 2004
Fallujah

THE LAVA DOGS told me they'd found the little outlaw here at the compound when they stormed the place, and the reason he was still here was that they didn't know what else to do with him. Since they'd decided to use the compound as the command post, and since this starving five-week-old puppy was already there, the choices were either to put him out on the street, execute him, or ignore him as he slowly died in the corner. The excuses they gave me were as follows:

"Not me, man, no way."

"Not worth the ammo."

"I ain't some kind of sicko, man."

In other words, they had enough pictures already from Fallujah to torture them slowly for the rest of their lives; they didn't need any more. Warriors, yes — puppy killers, no.

The puppy is named Lava, and while I'd like to say my comrades are creative enough to name him for symbolic reasons — like, you know, if they save him, they save themselves — I'm fairly sure they just couldn't come up with anything else.

Lava is the newest grunt, de-flea'd with kerosene, de-wormed with chewing tobacco, and pumped full of MREs.

Just so you understand how tough Lava really is: MREs, officially called "Meals Ready to Eat" but unofficially called "Meals Rejected by Everyone," are trilaminate retort pouches containing exactly twelve hundred calories of food, a plastic spoon, and a flameless heater that mixes magnesium and iron dust with salt to provide enough heat to warm the entrée. On the package, the meals state that "Restriction of food and nutrients leads to rapid weight loss, which leads to: Loss of strength, Decreased endurance, Loss of motivation, Decreased mental alertness," which supposedly coaxes us into at least opening the pouch to see what's inside.

Lava can't get enough of them, though, and learns real quick how to tear open pouches designed with three-year shelf lives that can withstand parachute drops of 1,250 feet or more.

Still, the best part is how these Marines, these elite, well-oiled machines of war who in theory can kill another human being in a hundred unique ways, become mere mortals in the presence of a tiny mammal. I'm shocked to hear a weird, misty tone in my fellow Marines' voices, a weird, misty look in their eyes, and weird, misty words that end in *ee*.

"You had yuckee little buggees all over you when we found you, huh? Now you're a brave little toughee. Are you our brave little toughee? You're a brave, little toughee, yessiree."

And the whole time Lava knows I've got him pegged, and he's stealing glances at me to make sure I see how he's soaking it all up.

The Marines brag about how the puppy attacks their boots and sleeps in their helmets and gnaws nonstop on the wires from journalists' satellite phones up on the roof. They tell me he can almost pick up an ammo belt. They tell me he loves M&M's.

"Did anyone feed Lava this morning?" someone yells out as "I did" comes back from every guy in the room.

He's like a cartoon character on fast-forward, always chasing something, chewing something, spinning head-on into something.

He stalks shadows and dust balls and pieces of balled-up paper. He can eat an entire cigar in less than two minutes and drag a flak jacket all the way across the floor. I mean, the little shit never stops. If you aren't dragging him along after you as he hangs on to your bootlaces with his teeth, he's up on the roof tangled in wires or lost and wailing in the bowels of somebody's backpack.

You can't yell at him, either, because even though you are an elite, well-oiled machine of war who in theory can kill another human being in a hundred unique ways, you'd still be considered a freak if you yelled at a puppy. He's completely pampered, kept warm, his sticks never thrown out of his sight range so his ego isn't damaged when he can't find them. I find it all pathetic. At first.

But the newest recruit already knows the two most important rules of boot camp by the time I come around: You don't chew on bullets and you only pee outside.

It's like Lava is everyone's kid. It gives them something to be responsible for above and beyond protecting their country and one another, and getting their brains blown out or worse in the process. He gives them a routine. And somehow, I become part of it.

○

Every morning we feed Lava his rehydrated Country Captain Chicken with Buttered Noodles and then pile out of the house to various posts across the city. Some Marines patrol the streets, some clear buildings looking for weapons, and some get killed and don't do much of anything after that.

Me, I have to patrol the streets with three wide-eyed Iraqi soldiers who, in their brand-new, US-issued, chocolate-chip cammies, wave their rifles around as if clearing the way of spiderwebs. Most still haven't figured out how to keep their rifles safely locked.

They are untrained, out of shape, and terrified. They're members of the Iraqi Armed Forces (IAF)—stouthearted doublespeak for "conquered and unemployed"—who were coaxed by the United States to help root out insurgents in Fallujah before the upcoming national elections.

Several days before we bombed the city, the new Iraqi recruits reported to Camp Fallujah, a few miles southeast of the city, with plenty of promising bravado. When Prime Minister Iyad Allawi made a surprise visit to the camp and urged them to be brave, to go forth and "arrest the killers" in Fallujah, the young Iraqi soldiers cried back with newly developed devil-dog gusto, "May they go to Hell!"

Things deteriorated quickly, though. First we built a tent camp for them just outside the walled safety of the main camp. We called it the East Fallujah Iraqi Camp and hoped the name and the handful of American advisers and liaison officers who also stayed there would boost their courage. The Iraqi soldiers endured both regular mortar shelling of their tents by insurgents and verbal bombardments from the Americans who only had one week to prepare them for their first-ever combat experience. So they were prone to the jitters and often woke up in the middle of the night shooting their un-safed rifles wildly. Thank God they didn't know how to aim.

It didn't help that influential Iraqi clerics publicly threatened the IAF soldiers with banishment to Hell, and the insurgent council that controlled Fallujah promised to behead any one of them who entered the city to "fight their own people." In a statement issued by the council just before we attacked, the insurgents stated: "We swear by God that we will stand against you in the streets, we will enter your houses and we will slaughter you just like sheep."

More than two hundred Iraqi troops quickly "resigned," and another two hundred were "on leave." My job now is to babysit some of the few who remain.

○

One afternoon about a week after I arrived at the compound, a few other Marines and I are patrolling one of the main streets with them. We're in front of a mosque, right? And they're all bug-eyed and waving their guns around and I'm a little strung out myself about what's going on around us only I can't let on, because I'm their example of what they're supposed to do and feel and be. But they're so freaked out, they're clearly about to shoot me or one of the other Marines by accident, so I figure the best thing is to make them more afraid of me than they are of the streets—you know, take their minds off it for a little while—so I start yelling.

"Knock that shit off."

And I keep yelling.

"Safe your weapons."

And they keep jerking their eyes one way and their rifles another way.

"I *said* knock that shit off!"

Until I see they've gone into another zone of fear that even I don't have access to, and one of the other Marines, I don't remember who, Tim O'Brien, Dan Doyle, or Mark Lombard, says to me, "Take it easy on them, man, they don't understand English," which kind of ruins my whole show.

"Yeah, well, they *better* learn fast." But I stop yelling and give them a look instead.

Then something rips past us in the air and we freeze. Just like that. It comes from nowhere but explodes a few yards away. Now we're moving fast. Fast.

A second rocket-propelled grenade (RPG) comes screaming our way, and I assess the situation in staccato—taking fire from two directions; small arms, medium machine gun, and rocket-propelled grenades; two men wounded; Iraqi soldiers running for cover; outnumbered in more ways than one.

I maneuver behind the hood of the Humvee to direct the men as Tim O'Brien, up in the turret, opens up with the MK-19 turret gun laying down a base of covering fire so the rest of us can position to fight.

Dan Doyle picks up a squad automatic weapon and fires toward the southwest.

Tim's a primary target in the turret, especially when his MK-19 jams and he has to fight with his M4—a shortened version of the M16A4 assault rifle—while he's trying to clear the MK-19 and make it ready to fire again. But it's Dan who gets hit. Blood runs down the inside of his left leg.

"Dan, get into that mosque," I order, but he ignores me and takes off running to get the Humvees positioned so we can evacuate the rest of the wounded, including Mark Lombard, who's bleeding all over the place but is on the radio calling in our situation report anyway.

Bullets and shrapnel ricochet from the hood of the Humvee inches to my right. Blood soaks Dan's pant leg.

"Get your ass into that mosque," I yell again, but he, get this, looks over at me and grins.

"Just a flesh wound."

Two armor-piercing rounds hit the vehicle and tear through its quarter-inch steel plate easier than needles through skin. I fire my M16A2 and yell for the Iraqi soldiers to direct their fire to the south.

Only I don't see them. Where the hell are they? I have to get the wounded to safety, so when I see them from the corner of my eye crouched numb between two overturned vehicles, I realize we're on our own.

I abandon my M16A2 for a more powerful squad automatic weapon, then run in front of the Humvee and fire away to the south. This apparently inspires one of the Iraqi soldiers to stick his head out, fire two rounds quickly—using me as his cover—and then duck back in. It's the last I see of the Iraqis for the rest of the thirty-minute fight.

○

At night we all gather back at the compound, where we cover the windows with blankets and sandbags, clean our weapons, and make sure Lava has something for dinner that he didn't have the night before.

Then the time comes when you have to put back on all your gear, ready your weapon, and sneak out to the portable toilets down the block. We call them porta-shitters. One of my greatest fears during the weeks I stay at the compound is the possibility of being blasted by an RPG in a porta-shitter.

If you survive that, then you bed down and smoke cigars and review the day's events with everyone else who made it.

"We found a weapons cache in that old UN food-for-oil place . . ."

"Yeah, well, we got caught in an alley . . ."

"Yeah, well, we had to transport wounded and they actually fell out of the Humvee onto the street when we got hit with an RPG or something we never saw coming."

They have nothing on me, though.

"Yeah, well, my Iraqi guys decided to take their naps during a firefight . . ."

As we talk, Lava climbs up and over our boots, destroys packages of M&M's, and paws through our blankets for prey.

"They don't have a clue out there . . ."

Then the puppy finds my lap and sits between my crossed legs staring out at the other Marines.

"I mean, how do DC brass ever expect to get these guys to secure their country if we're doing it all for them?"

I untie my boots, and Lava bites at the laces.

"I swear I am going to accidentally shoot the whole group of them if they don't shape up."

As I pull a boot off, the puppy grabs hold of the lace and tugs. I tug back. The puppy growls. I growl back.

"Hey, what's with this puppy anyway?" I ask. "What are you guys planning on doing with him?"

No one answers. Then one of the Marines stretches and yawns and says he's turning in. Others grunt. Lava crawls out of my lap and turns a few circles, flops down, and falls asleep with his nose buried in my empty boot.

Meanwhile, outside on the streets, psychological operations teams blast AC/DC and Jimi Hendrix through loudspeakers, with the additional sound effects of crying babies, screaming women, screeching cats, and howling dogs, in hopes of turning the insurgents' nerves to shreds. They broadcast insults in Arabic, including "You shoot like goatherders" and "May all the ambulances in Fallujah have enough fuel to pick up the bodies of the mujahideen," which, along with the mortar, grenades, ceaseless rumbling of Humvees, and twenty different kinds of aircraft flying in precise layers over the city including helicopters, attack jets, and small, pneumatically launched spy drones that roam the skies beaming back images to base from automatic video cameras, create a kind of white noise that allows us all to sleep pretty soundly through the night.

○

I guess they didn't want to answer my question about Lava that night, because like everything else in Fallujah during the invasion, nothing but the immediate was worth thinking about. Really, there wasn't room in your head for anything but what was right in front of you or right behind you or right around the next corner. The future spanned one city block at most. Your dreams consisted of RPGs that missed; lifelong goals were met if you made it back to the compound at night.

So the guys probably weren't avoiding the subject of what would happen to Lava so much as they were ignoring it. There just wasn't any room. But jeez, when a puppy picks your boots to fall asleep in, you do start to wonder how he'll die.

See, I've been a Marine since 1992 when I transferred from the navy, and I know that the little guy is going to die. I knew it right away when I saw him in the hall—*this one won't make it*—just like you could look at some of the other guys and think *This one won't make it, because his one eye twitches* or *This one won't make it, because he parts his hair on the right instead of the left*—superstitious stuff like that, which you know doesn't make sense but oils your engine anyway. I was thinking *This one won't make it, because he's too damned cute.*

I'm also a lieutenant colonel, which means I know military rules as well as anyone, and every time I picked Lava up, they darted across my brain like flares: *Prohibited activities for service members under General Order 1-A include adopting as pets or mascots, caring for or feeding any type of domestic or wild animals.*

CHAPTER THREE

May 2005
Denver, Indiana

KEN LICKLIDER THREW some more clothes into his suitcase and checked his watch. Right place, right time. Be there. That was the trick. Had been all his life.

The war raged and business was good—so good in fact that Ken, who'd been in Iraq and Afghanistan five times during the past two years, had trouble finding enough good people to work for him. He hoped the ad on his Web site—"Opportunities for Explosive Detector Dog handlers—overseas deployment in Iraq and Afghanistan—excellent pay"—would do the trick, but the added disclaimer "Must be able to obtain security clearance" would weed out a bunch.

It wasn't even the disclaimer that worried Ken so much. Plenty of people applied and plenty could probably get clearance, but you couldn't just let every alpha wannabe into the fold no matter how desperate you were to find employees. He'd learned that the hard way. Since opening Vohne Liche Kennels in 1993, he'd seen and rejected more than his share of yahoos.

While part of his success came from knowing how to find good dogs—he used German shepherds, Dutch shepherds, Belgian Malinois, and Labradors from all over the world—the biggest part of his success came from knowing how to find the right handlers. Most of his guys were former military police, security specialists and civilian police officers, tough guys—one of them used to manage a prison, and another was an undercover cop who specialized in outlaw motorcycle gangs—but in order to work for him, they had to have level heads. Had to get through the training. Had to find the discipline to handle his dogs, who weren't trained to attack on instinct but on focused, well-reasoned commands.

He trained his bomb-sniffing dogs in Iraq, for instance, to be "passive responders," which meant that when they detected the odor, landed the lottery, found what they'd been looking for all their lives, they didn't go wild and foam at the mouth; they just sat down and stared. Couldn't even wiggle their butts.

His handlers also had to have enough control of themselves to give control over to their dogs. That was a tough one, because a lot of these guys were control freaks out of professional necessity. Learning how to give that away was like learning how to shoot all over again.

But most importantly, Ken's handlers had to love dogs as much as he did. Like David Mack, his overseas program coordinator in Baghdad. Or Brad Ridenour, a former student who worked in Iraq for Triple Canopy Security. Now, there were two guys who understood the meaning of violence: Study it; avoid it when possible; then get back to taking care of your dog.

You were lucky if you knew that much, lucky if you took care of your dog before you took care of the bad guys, lucky if you understood that the dog would end up saving your life in more ways than one.

Ken was lucky. Hell, he was charmed. He'd started in dogs back in '77 with the air force as a police service trainer and handler and realized right away that the dogs watched over your sanity. At first he figured it was the focus being a good trainer and handler required that kept your mind from veering, but through the years—through the Secret Service work, through protecting presidents, foreign dignitaries, the Pan Am Games, and the pope with his dogs and handlers—Ken learned it was more than that. When you spent your entire career on the fringes of violence, the dogs helped remind you that you were still human.

He checked his watch one more time.

CHAPTER FOUR

November 2004
Fallujah

Anne Garrels tells me she sleeps pretty well at the command post. At least there's a roof over her head and a place to set up her satellite equipment, even though keeping Lava from chewing on the wires is just one of this war's pop quizzes for which she hasn't adequately prepared.

I say *this war* because she's attended several. Chechnya, Bosnia, Kosovo, Israel, Saudi Arabia, Afghanistan, the former Soviet Union, Central America, Tiananmen Square, Pakistan . . . you name it, she was there.

Anne's a trip. She can smoke, drink, and swear as well as any of us, knows more about war than any of us, and cares less about consequences than any of us, but here's the weird part: Put Lava in front of her, and she kind of falls apart at the seams.

"He's adorable," she says as the puppy gnaws away at thousands of dollars' worth of her radio broadcast equipment, "just adorable," and all the while she's transforming into a soft, feminine girl-next-door type whom you suddenly wish wasn't married.

But Anne is tougher than she looks. When she first entered the city as an embedded journalist for National Public Radio with Bravo

Company, First Battalion, Third Marine Regiment, she didn't have a sleeping bag because it was just one more thing to lug around—her broadcast equipment alone weighed fifty pounds. So she slept on the ground for minutes at a time, until bombs or falling bricks or blasts from sniper fire jolted her awake again. I mean, sleeping on the ground in the cold comes in a close second to sitting in full uniform on a porta-shitter worrying about death in terms of lousy ways to spend your time as far as I'm concerned, and she just shrugged it off with something like "Yeah, I'm a little tired."

But then in the compound she finds one of Lava's turds on her socks, and her eyes get misty like she's about to weep, and she says, "Isn't that adorable?" and is suddenly the girl next door again.

Anne isn't like the other reporters—who are usually guys and thus prone to all sorts of issues, not the least of which is preserving their masculinity as they piss in their pants. I mean, I do have to give them credit. They didn't come to Iraq in uniform and yet day after day they hump along after us, dodge the same RPGs as us, eat the same MREs as us, and all the while scribble their notes and whisper into their recorders and try like hell to seem nonchalant.

But not Anne. She flat-out admits that Fallujah scares the hell out of her. If one of the guys said that, we'd probably smirk and spit and examine our tattoos while saying some tough bullshit thing or another, but when Anne says it, it kind of eases some of the tension the rest of us are feeling. Because if all this fazes her, then at least we aren't the closet cowards we all secretly worry we are.

It's like she deserves to say it. She spends her days moving behind Bravo Company block by block, house by house, through a booby-trapped inferno as the army psychological operations teams broadcast their tapes over the mosque loudspeakers. It gets to her after a while, right? So as she moves through the narrow streets, she focuses solely on what lies directly ahead, or just above or around the next corner, sweating almost out loud about what comes next. And when she describes it, your insides scream *What a coincidence!* because you know exactly what she's talking about, and you almost feel obliged to bow.

So when Lava farts or Lava pees on somebody's boot or Lava shreds someone's only pair of underwear and Anne bends down and scoops him up and tells him how brave he is, we all kind of feel okay thinking so, too.

○

One of the things that I think worries Anne the most is that she's not telling her radio audience the real story about us. She complains about it a lot. How can you explain how lethal, how faulty, how fundamentally lousy the whole situation is here in general?

". . . chaotic . . . ," she reports, ". . . moments of sheer terror . . ."

She tries, but she always feels she misses the mark by a few inches.

I understand better than anyone that there are no words to adequately describe how the insurgents seem to communicate with one another and coordinate their attacks through a series of underground tunnels that run from mosque to mosque, and how, like some freakish version of a video game, the snipers pop up out of nowhere—on rooftops, in alleyways, from behind mosque walls—and you only stay alive to play another round by shooting them immediately wherever they pop out.

". . . rarely saw insurgents up close, just outlines through their night-vision scopes; the scurry of feet on rooftops above . . ."

Or how, without a sleeping bag, the cold night air magnifies the convulsive jitters that plague you after a while, so when you wake up one morning to find a Marine's poncho draped over you with no one claiming responsibility, you think how at this moment, in this place, in this real-time, hellish virtual video game of hide-and-go-seek, a cashmere blanket holds nothing over a dirty Marine poncho.

She doesn't even bother with that one.

○

We sit up at night in the compound and talk by the glow of the light sticks used to avoid detection by insurgents. We talk a lot, Anne and me, and usually Lava snuffles around us and plays cute, pretending not to listen, but he's taking it all in, I can tell, because every once in a while, when the conversation gets tough and I start, like, talking about something I normally don't and can't find the right way to de-scribe what I've seen or what I've done or what somebody else did and just stop talking, Lava looks up at me and cocks his little head as if waiting—I swear—for the rest of it. So I shrug and finish the story.

Like, the light sticks glow on our faces while everything else around us is dark, so we're on the moon, right?—a million miles away from our gods, our rules, our lives, and I hear my voice plowing through every roadblock and checkpoint without halting, because there's nothing, no gods, no rules, no lives standing guard to stop it.

". . . parents hate me being in the military, wanted me to be a doctor . . ."

". . . the marriage didn't work out . . ."

". . . sure, I want to be a dad someday . . ."

Anne listens and smokes and nods and smokes some more while we talk in the dim glow, and I never worry that she'll turn around and use anything I tell her in one of her radio stories. And I tell her some stuff.

". . . the first guy I killed . . ."

". . . found this baby in the rubble . . ."

". . . his face just exploded . . ."

She seems more focused on the stories of the younger guys any-way, the twenty-year-old grunts just in from basic training who walk around acting tough, like this is no big thing, like they've done this all their lives even though FREAKED OUT blinks on and off across their foreheads in neon. I think she feels sorry for them. She never says that, but that's what a lot of her stories home are about in the end.

Like the story she did about the initial bombing of Fallujah, as they waited on the outskirts of the city for the invasion to begin, when she realized how different this assignment was from any she'd been through before. Unlike the initial offensive against Iraq, for example, when aloof bombings killed anonymous enemies in uniform, this assault turned defensive as soon as it began. The enemy wasn't a soldier hired to shoot back anymore; he was now a civilian who hated you so much he'd down his breakfast, walk out of the house, and then blow himself up in your face.

Most of the Marines in Bravo Company had been in Iraq only two weeks when they convoyed to Fallujah where the new enemy, in a white Suburban van, introduced himself by careening into their seven-ton ammunition-laden truck, taking eight of them with him to wherever young warriors go when they're burned alive.

A few days later Anne interviewed a Marine psychologist sent in to offer counseling, who said the surviving members of Bravo Company didn't feel the expected anger or guilt nearly as much as a sense of disgrace.

"They experienced horrible shame of being helpless," he told her. "Marines hate above everything to be helpless, passive. It's not the way they see themselves, and it makes it hard for them to get back the feeling of confidence."

Anne knew the feeling, but none of it compared with the sense of professional disability she felt in Fallujah. How could you possibly report to people thousands of miles away how perverse it seemed to toss kids a sense of their own mortality with the casualness of a softball?

"Most had yet to experience combat . . . ," she reported. "Soon they would know."

They weren't adults, most were old-ish teenagers, so for Anne, humping along after them was like trying to follow a pack of adolescent pit bulls previously chained up for too many days. Most had just left home—left rented video games, first cars, and part-time jobs—to defend, against all enemies foreign and domestic, the Constitution of the United States even though many would be hard-pressed to tell you what was actually in the thing.

Was that enough? Would people back home get it? She could just come out and say it—*They're too young to be dealing with this, folks. They aren't ready for this, folks. They only just learned to ride bikes, for God's sake, folks*—but she wondered if it would bother anyone for any meaningful period of time.

"They wanted more from life than what they had back home. They believed the Marines when they said, *You can be the best*."

But she hoped she snared it when she interviewed one young grunt and asked him what his mission was here in Fallujah.

"Kill the enemy, man," he said into her microphone. "Kill the enemy, that's about it."

○

I don't let Lava sleep with me at first. I always scoot him off toward Anne or somebody else more willing to sleep with a snoring piglet who farts MREs all night.

Then one night Anne says to me, "He's so adorable. What's going to happen to him?"

I give the shrug. "Dunno."

Another night we're talking and she tells me she's scheduled to go back to the States in a few weeks. Lava bounces around on our sleeping bags.

"Good for you." I smile and roll Lava onto his back and scratch his belly until his back paws quiver.

"Then I'm coming back to report on the elections from Baghdad."

I nod and stare down at the puppy, who provides a convenient diversion from eye contact as I tell her that I'm scheduled to rotate out in April sometime. I feel guilty about it. About leaving. But I don't tell her.

"I imagine you're happy about that."

"Sure."

"So what's going to happen to Lava?"

I turn the puppy upright and nudge him away.

"Who knows?"

Lava rushes back, grabs one of my bootlaces, and tugs.

"He is so cute."

"Yep."

I push Lava away again. The puppy turns and faces me as he bends his front legs down and pushes his rear end into the air. He wags his tail and barks. Then he rushes the boots again.

"Cut it out."

So I shove him away, right? I suddenly don't want the little shit chewing on my boots anymore.

"What will you do when you get home?"

Lava regroups and charges.

"Not sure yet."

This time I really push him away, let him know what's what, and he loses his balance and his legs give out while he makes little squeaks of terror and rolls several times across the floor.

"Oh man."

I mean, I can't begin to explain how bad I felt about this. I mean, really bad. You know, I just shoved a little puppy across the floor. So I pull Lava back toward me and scratch the bridge of his nose. He looks up at me all tough and wags his tail like it's no big deal.

"Hey, sorry."

But I feel like shit and let him sleep on my poncho that night, and I think that's how Anne finds her story.

During the fighting, the battalion gained a new member, a tiny puppy they named Lava Dog . . . Though filthy themselves, they've lovingly washed him down to get rid of the sand fleas.

He sleeps nestled in a Marine poncho.

CHAPTER FIVE

November 2004
Fallujah

GENERAL ORDER 1-A is taken pretty seriously by the military. No pets allowed. That's because they've invested a lot of time and money into trashing your moral clarity, and they don't want anything like compassion messing things up. Your job is to shoot the enemy, period, and if anything close to compassion rears its ugly head, you better shoot that down, too, or you're in some deep, scary shit.

None of us talks about what will happen to Lava, because it means making decisions we don't want to make for reasons we're not being paid to consider in the first place. Frankly, it's easier to just go blow stuff up.

Most nights Lava sleeps outside on the roof of the compound with a group of the BLT 1/3 Marines, but once the weather turns colder, he comes inside at night. That's when he starts bugging me, hanging around looking wide-eyed and cute, all paws and snuffles and innocence.

In reality, when he isn't asleep, he's anything but innocent. I personally saw the little monster destroy several maps, two pairs of boots, one cell phone, photographs of someone's kids, five pillows, and some grunt's only pair of socks.

○

One morning I wake up and find Lava sitting near my sleeping bag staring at me, with his left ear flapped forward and the remains of a toothpaste tube stuffed in his mouth.

"Morning," I say.

He replies with a minty belch and then barfs up standard-issue Colgate all over my sleeping bag.

○

In addition to forbidding pets, General Order 1-A also prohibits any conduct that is "prejudicial to the maintenance of good order and discipline of all forces," meaning that anything that diminishes morale or discipline is banned. This includes drinking alcohol in countries that don't allow it, entering religious sites without special orders, the theft or destruction of archaeological artifacts, and the taking of souvenirs. Anything that bargains with a Marine's discipline, anything that toys with his ability to shoot and shoot well, has to be censored.

I know what's what in that department. During World War II only 15 percent of the troops actually fired at their enemies in battle, because most of them didn't want to kill anyone. The problem is that sticky moral compass that discourages human beings from killing other human beings, so over the years the smart guys devised ways to overcome any and all ethical thorns, because not wanting to kill the enemy in combat posed, well, problems. Effective warriors, they decided, had to be trained without regard to moral repercussions.

So after World War II Marines were trained to act immediately and reflexively rather than to stop and think about it first. Through the use of Pavlovian conditioning, we were taught to kill on command. Instead of shooting at the old-time bull's-eye targets, we were taught to shoot at human-silhouette-shaped targets that popped up out of nowhere, and the repeated use of pop-up marksmanship ranges combined with fire commands, battle drills, and continued orders to "Shoot!" from authority figures not only controlled our reactions but anesthetized them as well. By the time the Vietnam War rolled around, 90 percent of American troops fired at the adversary. Now killing was as reflexive as answering a phone when it rang, and nothing was supposed to interfere with progress. Nothing.

○

Another morning I wake to see Lava's entire front end stuffed into one of my boots with his butt and back legs draped out over the side. He's not moving, right? So I think he's dead.

"Oh shit."

Probably from the MREs.

"Oh no. Oh shit."

Lava's body doesn't move at first, but when he hears my voice, his tail starts waving like a wind-kissed flag, and I decide that from now on, he's not eating any more noodles, biscuits, or beans in butter sauce. No more M&M's. No more toothpaste. Only meat. That's what real dogs eat, meat.

○

Out on the streets one day during that first week, I discover the Iraqi soldiers with looted candy bars and cigarettes in their pockets, and because we're supposed to train them to be just like us—moral except for the killing stuff—and because looting breaks all the rules, I decide to give them a little additional training.

I pace the ground six inches in front of them with an unopened candy bar clenched in my fist. They wince and lean back.

"Well, excuuuuse me, am I invading your personal space?" I say through the interpreter, letting concern drip like battery acid from every word, because, you know, I have to make an impression here.

The three soldiers try not to move, but their eyes swivel back and forth between me and the interpreter, who is the closest thing they can trace back to the good old days when everyone spoke Arabic and no one yelled at them for eating a little candy.

"Well, I have some information for you pathetic excuses for soldiers." I push my face into exhale range of one of the men and deliver a jab to his chest with each word.

"You have no personal space."

I step back and stare at the unopened candy bar in my hand as if it just fell from a spaceship.

"What is this?"

The three soldiers eye the interpreter.

"And what are these?"

I march toward them, yank packs of cigarettes and more candy bars from their vests, and throw them on the ground with as much passion as I can muster. The soldiers look at the interpreter, down at the loot, and back at the interpreter again.

"Did you *pay* for this stuff?"

The three nod in unison.

"Which *one* of you paid for it?"

The three point to one another simultaneously.

They just don't get it. These guys are supposed to take over their country's security, and here they are acting like the Three Stooges. Disobeying orders threatens survival out here, and while just about everything threatens survival out here including walking, talking, and pissing in the wrong place, lack of discipline is up near the top of the list of sure killers, along with panic, loss of focus, and too much compassion.

"*You are less than men for stealing.*"

I pace up and down in front of the soldiers.

"*You humiliate yourselves and the Iraqi forces.*"

I spit at their feet.

"*You are no good as soldiers and I will abandon you here in Fallujah, where you will be beheaded by insurgents.*"

I rip off my helmet.

"*You are nothing but shit.*"

The interpreter stops and looks at me.

"Go on, translate *shit*. It's not *that* hard."

I throw my helmet on the ground.

"Repeat after me. *I do not steal.*"

The soldiers mumble their response to the interpreter.

"*In English. I do not steal.*"

"In inglezee. I do not sti-il."

"*I do not lie.*"

"I do not lie."

"*I am a moron and I worship the ground you walk on, sir.*"

Discipline overrides everything between Heaven and earth here, including hunger, exhaustion, fear, homesickness, empathy, guilt, hangovers, snipers, regret, hatred, intestinal blockage, thoughts of suicide, calls to prayer, and letters from home.

"*And from this time forth, thy righteous ordinance of discipline will be my guide and I will forgo sex, kill my firstborn, chew with my mouth closed, take no prisoners, do unto others, brush in back, worship my gun, place I before E except after C, leave no Marine behind, oo-rah, praise the Lord, hail Caesar full of grace, Santa Claus lives, Allah is great, yes sir, always and forever and ever and ever, amen.*"

Poor schmucks. They start praying. They don't even hear me anymore because they're whispering "Allah, Allah" and trying not to cry, only I see they aren't looking at me anymore but at something behind my back.

I glance across the street and at first only see the usual horizon of a city blown to smithereens. Then I see something moving, and I stiffen and position my gun.

"Allah, Allah."

It takes me a second to focus.

I squint and grip the gun, because my palms start sweating, and my fingers start shaking, and the soldiers keep moaning, and I scream "Shut the *fuck* up," because I can't hold the rifle steady anymore, because what I see is a pack of dogs . . . "Allah, Allah" . . . feeding on meat, "Oh God," and I think I'm going to puke.

○

Another morning I wake up thinking someone short-sheeted my sleeping bag because I can't push my feet to the end. It's Lava, who managed to crawl in during the middle of the night and curl up at the bottom in a ball.

"Oh man. This has got to stop."

He snores away, and I don't want to disturb him because it's still too early to get up, so as I lie there enjoying the warmth of his breath on my feet, General Order 1-A starts tangoing around in my head.

Prohibited activities for service members under General Order 1-A include adopting as pets or mascots, caring for or feeding any type of domestic or wild animals. While most of the Marines sleeping around me would admit that it feels good to finally do what they've been trained to do, they don't feel so good about it feeling so good. All the rules and training prove valuable out here, but what the hell do you do with yourself later?

I know what will happen to them later. They won't sleep much, they'll experience panic attacks, they'll avoid their neighbors, they'll drink, they'll snort, they'll shoot, they'll binge on emotional numbness, and that's only if they find some kind of counseling that talks them out of feeling so different from everybody else even though they are different from everybody else.

I tried. I tried breaking the rules once by leaving the fold, when the adrenaline rushes of carrier-arrested landings, airborne operations, and rappelling from helicopters faded and left me itching from the inside out. All the training was fine, all the discipline was great, but what did I do with myself at the end of the day?

When I left active duty, I joined the civilian world working counternarcotics with the US Attorney's office in San Diego, then wandered into an Internet start-up in Newport Beach as an officer of the company, and then into Salomon Smith Barney as a financial consultant.

But it never felt normal. It was like *There has to be more than this.* What's the point? What are the objectives? What in the hell are the *rules*?

Then the attacks on 9/11 kickboxed being normal to a pulp, and I returned to active duty as soon as I could. I deployed with the Eleventh Marine Expeditionary Unit (Special Operations Capable) to Kuwait and Jordan. Then I deployed to Operation Iraqi Freedom in February 2003 and, by August, found myself assigned as the Special Forces liaison officer for the First Marine Expeditionary Force in Qatar. My third deployment in two years swept me into Camp Fallujah, where I trained the Iraqi Special Forces who are now out here on the streets of this godforsaken ghost town watching stray dogs eat their dead countrymen.

But it feels normal. Despite the bombs and the insurgents and the rubble, it feels like I belong here. And how screwed up is that?

I reach down into the sleeping bag and pull Lava up under my chin. He snorts and snuffles around, and I start scratching his ears.

"What's going to happen to you once we leave, little guy?"

The puppy opens one eye and stares up at me, and I start thinking the stuff we're not supposed to think—about how we're either going to have to shoot him or abandon him on the streets here in Fallujah where for dogs, eating human flesh is normal.

Lava's eyes lower to half-mast as his head drops slowly backward. I blow lightly on his face, because I don't want to be awake alone. His eyes pop open. He looks annoyed.

"What, am I invading your personal space?"

He thumps his tail on my chest.

"Well, you are invading mine."

CHAPTER SIX

May 2005
In flight from Kirkuk to Baghdad

Brad Ridenour figured he owed Ken Licklider this favor. Helping Ken help a Marine wasn't the only reason he was flying from the US/ British embassy in Kirkuk to Baghdad International Airport, but it was up at the top of the list. That and going home.

After four months in Iraq working as a dog handler for Triple Canopy Security, Brad was ready for the break — all the guys were — and while any of them would have helped Ken out on this, Brad was the obvious volunteer. After all, this was only his first tour of Iraq, so he didn't *need* to get home as much as the guys who'd been at this for a while.

But he did need a break. Home seemed like another story, where once upon a time he'd been a police officer in the small town of Portland, Indiana, and where, before he became the department's K9 handler after training under Ken at Vohne Liche Kennels, the plot sat as stagnant as a Midwest slough. But it wasn't the need for more drama that cornered Brad into going to Iraq. And it wasn't Ken's last-minute call asking him if he wanted the job with Triple Canopy. It was the fact that once he'd teamed up with his dog, Vischa, at Vohne Liche Kennels and spent several months learning to communicate with another species, he'd decided that not even communicating with extraterrestrials could offer more reward. He loved working with dogs. Ken's contract with Triple Canopy Security, which had a contract with the US State Department to guard high-risk embassies in Iraq, provided Brad the chance to do it for a living.

But it was a hell of a way to make a living. He'd lost fifty pounds in the past four months. The first ten came off from just getting into the country, when he'd learned how fidgety Iraqi customs officers could be. He traveled with another dog handler, and while Brad got Vischa through without a hitch, when the customs officials looked at the other handler's papers and then at his dog's health certificate, they demanded that the dog's photograph be taken. The other handler had to pick up the ninety-pound German shepherd and hold him eye level with the camera. Brad didn't understand what security measures were sealed by having the dog's picture taken and didn't ask, but it served notice of things to come.

The next ten pounds came off during his first month at Triple Canopy's fortified compound at the edge between the Green and Red Zones of Baghdad.

Because the US military was stretched to its breaking point, the private company won government contracts in 2004 to protect the thirteen headquarters of the Coalition Provisional Authority (CPA), which governed Iraq during the US-led occupation. The company, newly formed by two retired members of the US Army's Delta Force, shipped armored vehicles, weapons, and rucksacks full of cash to Iraq, where its employees used them to protect American dignitaries. Most of Triple Canopy's recruits came from Latin America, mostly from Peru, Chile, Colombia, and El Salvador, and while they didn't like to be called mercenaries, they probably could have pasted the word into their résumés if necessary.

Brad and Vischa's first job for Triple Canopy was to protect the company's compound in the Green Zone by checking incoming -vehicles for explosives. Only one bomb went off while he was there—an improvised explosive device (IED) detonated at the entrance of the Iraqi National Guard camp across a field from the Triple Canopy camp, but it was close enough to blind Brad when its shock wave sent a fine layer of dust his way.

The last thirty pounds came off one month at a time during the twelve weeks he spent searching for explosives at the entrance to the US/British Embassy in Kirkuk. It didn't seem like a long time when looking back, but wearing Kevlar 24/7, moving only in armored vehicles at high rates of speed, and holding your breath in every time a vehicle approached the embassy went a long way toward inciting homesickness. He'd held his breath so many times during the past four months, going home felt like gulping air.

But he had to do this one last thing for Ken.

CHAPTER SEVEN

November 2004
Fallujah

AFTER THREE WEEKS in Fallujah, I return to the main base with Lava on Thanksgiving Day in a Humvee—which, after serial bombardments, firefights, and crashes, looks more like a secondhand stock car than a High Mobility Multipurpose Wheeled Vehicle that costs slightly less to assemble than the average American mansion.

I have no idea what I'm going to do with Lava, but he loves the loud, rumbling trip, and as I drive and he perches on my lap and drools all over the window and *roos* at the thousands of Fallujah evacuees we pass by, I enter yet another excuse to the catalog of why I'm breaking military rules: I can't help it.

I don't remember exactly when the excuses started, but it was sometime between the afternoon I saw the dogs eating dead bodies and the time I found Lava rolled up in my sleeping bag. After that, the excuses flowed: because the Iraqi soldiers were failing; because I was tired; because so many children hadn't been evacuated by their parents when they'd been warned; because I was out of cigars; because I couldn't sleep at night anymore unless some little fur ball was nestled up against me and breathing on my feet. By the time I'm scheduled to leave Fallujah, I have so many excuses scattered around, I just roll them all up into one big ball of hazy justification and plop Lava in the Humvee.

I call friends and family back in the States and tell them about Lava and ask for help. I call on a cell phone, so I think at first that the silences on the other end are the usual international lag, but I realize, as the silences stretch out, that my friends are trying to place the word *puppy* within the context of words they have concerning me.

See, they're all scared that if I don't get killed, I'll lose my mind in Iraq and end up eating raw meat, collecting weapons, and sending anonymous scary letters to people I don't know. So when I tell them I have a puppy and then there's this long silence, I can sense them connecting the dots between who I was when I left and who they're terrified I'll be when I get back.

Like, when I call one of my best buddies back in San Diego, Eric Luna, and ask him if he knows how to get a dog out of Iraq, I hear nothing for a long time but some static.

"Hey, Easy E, you still there?"

"Yeah, man, I'm here. What did you just say?"

Talking between Iraq and California is expensive and often disrupted, so you have to say everything as quickly as you can. It's an art, and fashioning my explanation into an understandable form that begins with stolen candy and ends with stray dogs eating dead bodies only fuels Eric's worst fears.

"What?" he keeps saying, like he can't hear me.

"RPGs . . . MREs . . . M&M's . . ."

"What?"

". . . bloated bodies . . . bootlaces . . . satellite wires . . . psychological operations . . . we're not normal . . ."

"What?"

". . . and, see, there are these dangerous portable toilets . . ."

"*What?*"

"*Pup-py.* I have this *pup-py.* Can you help me figure a way to help me get him out of the country?"

Eric collects his wits and decides that in order to avoid future repercussions, the best thing to do is to agree.

"Sure, man. Yeah, anything you want."

○

The trip between the city and camp is only about twelve miles, but it's a pretty tricky stretch, and targeting a military convoy is easier than picking lice off a bald dog.

Contrary to sensible belief, the twenty thousand Humvees they have us driving around Iraq are not all armored vehicles. While their characteristics look cool on paper—weight: 5,200 pounds; engine: V8, 6.2-liter displacement, fuel-injected diesel, liquid-cooled, compression ignition; horsepower: 150 at 3,600 rpm—without armor, they are just big tin cans. We dress them up ourselves with sandbags, metal, and plywood, but that only weighs down the suspension and drivetrain components and creates more shrapnel when we're hit with an RPG or by a roadside bomb.

As a result, convoys make great targets, and in just one easy attack the insurgents can disrupt supply runs, mangle equipment, and butcher troops all at the same time. No suicide required. In fact, they're getting so good at setting off bombs from far away—igniting them with garage door openers, remote controls for toy cars, and beepers requiring only a cell phone call to set them off—using suicide bombers has almost become yesterday's fashion.

The enemy dangles soda cans from trees and packs explosives into roadkill. They hide bombs in girders, vegetated highway dividers, guardrails, trash cans, and manholes. They bury bombs in underground tunnels. They drop bombs from bridges. The convoy drivers keep a specific distance between their vehicles, usually fifty to a hundred meters depending on the dust factor, so the entire herd won't be taken down at once by a land mine.

When the convoy halts for equipment inspection or refueling, every driver stays in his vehicle with the motor running while every other eye scans the horizon 360 degrees and back again. Sometimes one of us will venture out to take a leak, but peeing on the side of the road in the middle of the Sunni Triangle isn't very safe; your chances of being hit are about as high as those for the fat boy in dodgeball.

If you *are* hit while peeing, the following advice is given in our *Lessons Learned* handbook: "RETURN FIRE—Extremely Effective; Continue to move; Do Not Stop!! They want you to do this; Do not be afraid to shoot; . . . anyone not stopping enemy activity is enabling the activity—This makes return fire morally right."

Usually before a convoy moves out, we gather at a staging site where the commander logs us in, the vehicles are inspected, personal items including clothes, food, and water are loaded, and heavy machine guns, grenade launchers, and other weapons are mounted, dusted, lubed, and readied to fire. The commander usually briefs us about new intelligence, the convoy route, radio call signs, and road-safety precautions, and follows with immediate action drills if the convoy gets hammered anyway. In our case we left the danger of Fallujah for the danger of the road by just piling things into the Humvees as fast as we could and exchanging good-luck salutes with the commander.

○

So we're driving along to the camp on a tricky road past all these Fallujah evacuees who now live in US-erected tents out in the cold and are pissed off about it. Like, they hate our guts.

The four of us in the Humvee make jokes about the old men in dresses and the fat women behind veils and egg on Lava when he barks.

"*Kill,*" we say and fall out laughing, because we think it's so damned funny. "Kill, Lava, *kill.*" We're nervous. It helps pass the time.

At first, as the convoy rolls past and the evacuees see this little puppy barking wildly at them through the Humvee's window, I expect them to give us the finger and shout nasty predictions about what will happen to us after we die. I expect any second to see one of the old guys pull a machine gun out of his robe and blast away as he's smiling. I expect burning effigies and hordes of shouting clerics with fists high in the air.

It's all a game really. Monopoly with bombs. Capture the Flag with grenades. See, there's this line that's drawn that's just meant to be crossed, and you stand on one side with your goods and they stand on the other with their goods, and the teams lob insults back and forth — "My stuff's better than yours!" "No, my stuff's better than yours!" "Well, I know the Referee!" "Oh, yeah? I'm *related* to the Referee" — until someone finally steps over the line and play officially begins.

I guess the Ref is the only one who really knows who crossed first and under what duress, but at this point everyone's so balled up in the name-calling — "Insurgents . . . murderers . . . terrorists . . . fanatics"; "Imperialists . . . infidels . . . invaders" — it doesn't matter anymore who did what or when.

Imagine the old Ref up there in the North Pole being all non-partisan and looking down on this. It's embarrassing. No wonder he doesn't show his face anymore.

And here we are driving by in our convoy past these people, and I can't stop thinking about the dogs. After a couple of days walking around the bodies in Fallujah, you got good at telling which ones the dogs had gotten to — the skin was shredded off the fattiest parts of their bodies, mostly the stomachs, butt cheeks, and soles of the feet — and that, my friend, is some gut-wrenching shit.

But they just stare at us. No rocks. No mutilated American flags. No calls to jihad with weapons raised in the air. Just stares, like they don't have energy to do anything else, mile after mile of them. After a while I start feeling like I've pulled off a brilliant practical joke that went too far and Lava's *rooing* starts getting to me.

"Come on, buddy, cut it out."

But he tears from one window to the other, and one of the other guys tells him to stop, and these faces stare at us through the dirty glass, but it's not funny anymore, and Lava just keeps *roo-roo-roooo-ing*, mile after mile, face after face, until I think my head is about to explode, "*Knock that shit off,*" and I slam on the brakes.

Lava stares at me. The guys stare at me. The faces, the people outside, stare at me. And they've got that look, all of them, that look that says *Caught your cool off guard, did we?* so I shrug it off, you know, recompose and grin and peel off real fast, leaving the Iraqis in a plume of dust and dirt.

Except as the mood in the Humvee gets back to normal, I can still feel Lava staring at me.

CHAPTER EIGHT

November 2004
Camp Fallujah

AS WE PULL through the gates of Camp Fallujah, the holiday scenery provides what you'd expect from an abandoned Iraqi military installation and former Iranian terrorist training camp taken over by US forces located midway between Baghdad and Fallujah, about eight thousand miles away from Plymouth Rock. Congested landing pads. Humvee graveyards. Rows of portable toilets making some civilian contractor lots and lots of money.

What I don't expect is all the activity at the Mortuary Affairs building with DO NOT ENTER posted at its doors. That's something new. It makes me think of Anne Garrels's stories. I hope she got out of the country okay.

At least the weather is cool, and after stuffing Lava in my backpack and sneaking him into my room in the officers' building, I turn on the heater to keep him warm.

"You okay in here, little guy?"

Lava looks up at me and cocks his head. As I stare down at this cute but fairly drastic breach of military law, I wonder if I've done the right thing. Lava will be vulnerable here at the camp, which under regulations can't harbor any dogs other than the military's working canines. As it is, stray dogs and cats swarm the camp looking for food, and rumor has it that they're being drowned in a nearby pond.

The officers' building is the *worst* place on base to hide a bouncing ball with vocal chords, but the need to decompress from the last three weeks drains me of incentive to do anything but sleep, so I pull Lava up on the cot next to me, where neither of us moves for the next nine hours.

I dream, though. Only I dream reality, can't get away from it, even in sleep.

I'm patrolling one of the main streets of Fallujah in front of a mosque and the Iraqi soldiers are waving their guns around and I'm yelling at them to safety their weapons and Tim O'Brien is telling me to take it easy on them, because they don't understand English.

And I turn on Tim and say "Well, they *better* learn fast," and he starts grinning and saying something, only suddenly his head isn't there anymore, it's on the ground, and grenades explode around us, and I grab up his head and try to jam it back onto the neck of his body, try to make it work again so I can hear what he has to say, only it's not sticking, so I try connecting the tendons from his neck to the tendons in his head only they're all tangled up and sticky and I can't put two and two together, and the grenades keep exploding, and then the eyes in the head in my hands start swiveling back and forth and the mouth starts spewing blood, but it's grinning, it's working, it's spewing and grinning and working and saying "It's only a flesh wound, man. It's only a flesh wound."

In the morning the bed is soaked, and Lava shivers under the covers drenched in his own pee. It's the first time this has happened since he started sleeping in my bag in Fallujah.

"Humiliated?"

He whimpers.

"Nightmares?"

Lava pushes his nose and then most of his body under the pillow. I hum the Marine anthem to him. His tail starts patting the bed.

"Me too."

○

I decide I'll risk talking to the dog handlers at the other end of the base where they actually grow green grass for the dogs to walk on. They treat the military working dogs well.

As in Delta Force or the navy SEALs, the working dogs make up an elite unit that outspecializes any weaponry or high-tech mapping systems the US armed forces possess. Several hundred thousand years of evolution make their noses stronger, their teeth sharper, and their legs faster than any human being alive. That's what the handlers tell me anyway.

Most are Belgian Malinois and German shepherds, and like the rest of us, each possesses his own military service record book and each learns to attack on command without thinking first. Before they ever arrive in Iraq, the trainers tell me that the working dogs attend boot camp at Lackland Air Force Base, where the Department of Defense maintains a high-tech veterinary hospital that includes specialists in pathology, internal medicine, surgery, radiology, and epidemiology who can perform fundus photography, endoscopy, arthroscopy, laser surgery, electrodiagnostics, hip replacements, fluoroscopy, and echocardiography in state-of-the-art clinical laboratories, dental suites, surgical areas, radiology areas, intensive care units, and anesthetic recovery rooms.

Boot camp for the working dogs consists of explosives detection and patrol, where they drill, they march, and they pace like any human recruit. The dogs learn the four classics—*sit*, *down*, *heel*, and *stay*—but the command *get him* is added to the syllabus as well. They learn to obey the commands in upwinds, downwinds, and crosswinds in addition to a variety of movements including march, rear march, column left, and column right.

Because of the large number of receptors in their noses and the large olfactory parts of their brains, the working dogs enhance the Marines' ability to detect faint odors and intruders by about a thousand times, with about 95 percent accuracy. A well-trained military dog can detect dynamite, detonator cords, sodium chloride, potassium chloride, time fuses, and smokeless powder.

When the dogs finish initial training, they're issued bulletproof camouflage vests that weigh seven pounds and cost about a thousand dollars each. The vests contain compartments for cold packs to prevent heatstroke and attachments that enable the dogs to be dropped by parachute or hauled up by rope.

Once equipped, the dog is paired with a handler. At Camp Fallujah, the two live and work together—they're rarely apart—and the dog and handler become so dedicated to each other that after two years, the dog is rotated out to keep the pair from becoming too attached. They trust each other to perfection. They know each other's breathing patterns. The bond between them is so strong that if a handler searches a suspect, and the suspect tries to hurt the handler, the dog attacks immediately without any command whatsoever. The dog then bites and holds the suspect down until he hears the command *out*, which means that if the handler is killed or knocked unconscious first, the dog will literally die holding the suspect down as he waits to receive orders to let go.

It therefore comes as no surprise to me when the dog handlers at Camp Fallujah smile and shake their heads when I ask if Lava can hide out in one of the kennels.

"Can't help you, sir . . ."

I'm equally unsurprised when they tell me the closest military veterinarian who can give Lava vaccinations works at a base in

Baghdad—some forty treacherous miles away—and because of General Order 1-A, they doubt he'll be able to help.

They wish me luck, though, and give me what I suspect is some very expensive dog food.

○

Back at the officers' building, I immediately e-mail the military veterinarian in Baghdad. I know it's a risk, but I hope the veterinarian is as understanding as the handlers here at camp.

"I found this puppy in Fallujah . . ."

Then I sit back and think about what the dog handlers told me when I asked what happens to the dogs when their tour of duty is over.

As with the Marines, it turns out, the military working dogs' elite status hurts them in the end. They aren't like other dogs, and since the canine warriors can't simply be debriefed, they have nowhere to go. If a military dog becomes physically unable to perform his tasks in the field—usually when he's about ten years old—a veterinarian deems him as either "nondeployable" or "stateside deployment only" and his military records are sent to Lackland to a full medical review board.

If a nondeployable dog is deemed "adoptable," meaning he probably won't storm local playgrounds and attack small children unprovoked, and if the potential adopter understands the possible risks, meaning he or she understands that small children might provoke the dog who might storm the playground and attack them, then the adopter signs an agreement that absolves the Department of Defense of any liability for damage or injury the dog might cause.

Most of them, though, are deemed nonadoptable. These are the dogs whose entire lives centered on carrying out orders to perfection, who were so devoted to the military, they obeyed to the death. These were the most faithful, dependable, patriotic dogs of the lot, so they're handed "final disposition" papers and euthanized.

I stare at the computer screen in front of me and try hard not to make comparisons. Nonadoptable. Maladjusted. Apt to attack small children on playgrounds. I bleed allegiance to the flag.

I follow my e-mail to the military veterinarian with an SOS to everyone but the gatekeepers of the Emerald City.

"I found this puppy in Fallujah . . ."

O

Later that day I receive word that I'm supposed to report to the Joint Task Force in Balad to replace a lieutenant colonel, Ignatius "Buck" Liberto, who's going on leave for six weeks. I know the guy, right? So I e-mail him in Balad and ask if he'll take Lava home with him when he leaves.

No problem from Buck's end, but he's flying out on a military plane, and in order to transport a puppy he'll need all of Lava's vaccination papers and approval from brass. I'm thinking that's no big deal until I get the response from the military veterinarian in Baghdad.

He respectfully reiterates General Order 1-A that prevents the Marines from keeping pets, and further points out that diseases such as leishmania, hydatid disease, and rabies are common among stray dogs in Iraq.

"My apparent lack of concern for this puppy isn't due to not caring. I'm simply following orders, regulations, and my desire to protect the public health of our soldiers," the veterinarian writes.

"What I'm trying to make clear, Sir, is that nothing we can do for you is going to assist you in getting the dog home."

Well, shit.

CHAPTER NINE

December 2004
Camp Fallujah

DUST SWIRLS IN the Humvee's headlights as it grumbles in low gear toward the far end of the base. Concrete bunkers, concertina wire, tents, and sandbags appear and disappear before me like quick thoughts, and I notice how much sharper the edges of things seem than when muted by all-out sun. Then again, everything seems weird when you can't sleep in the middle of the night.

It's weird that I'm driving across base. It's weird that it gets so cold in Iraq and that I'm crossing thin-skinned ice puddles under a black winter sky tattooed with stars. It's weird that the prefab metal buildings erected by the Iraqi Republican Guard to train terrorists are now surrounded by US-stuffed sandbags to keep them out. It's weird that the white beam of the headlight seems to stab with violence at whatever I'm passing—the chow hall, a big plastic tub used for Marines who decide to get baptized, a Humvee with a ram's skull roped to its front, the "Morale, Welfare and Recreation" building filled with PlayStation 2 consoles that the psychologists recommend we use to unwind. It's weird that there's war. It's weird that I'm part of it.

Where am I driving? To the Lava Dogs' building.

Why am I driving to the Lava Dogs' building? Because I can't sleep.

Why can't I sleep? Because Lava is in the Lava Dogs' building.

Now that they're back on base, it only seems natural that Lava should visit his uncles who conveniently live as far away from the officers' building as they can.

Only I can't sleep.

I start to nod off, but suddenly, like an alarm's going off, I think, *I've got to leave for Balad in two days*, followed by *Figure it out, Kopelman*, followed by *But how . . .* , followed by *Just figure the thing out*, followed by *Lava's going to get shot*.

See, orders just came down and the Department of Defense hired contractors to kill all nonmilitary dogs found on American bases in Iraq. Seems word got out about the stray dogs eating dead bodies, and while it's perfectly okay for us to make the bodies dead in the first place, it's not quite cool to have dogs walking around eating them. There's some fine line there I guess we're not supposed to notice. Maybe it has to do with cooties.

Anyway, it also turns out that I'm not the only loon who wants to get a dog out of Iraq. There are actually a lot of guys writing home looking for help. I mean, there were all these stories online about it, which I found while Googling "Iraq dogs out" and "Iraq puppy out" and that sort of thing. I was at a complete loss until I found the story about an army sergeant who said that his unit tried to get their dog back to the United States—but the "dog killers," he said, got her first. They hid her and fed her and then found someone going back to the States who would take her, but then at the last minute, as she was actually in the flight line ready to go and all the guys were saying good-bye, some jerk following orders comes up, yanks her away, and shoots her.

That's the kind of thing that makes you pause and wonder, What the *fuck*?

So I start Googling anything I can think of—puppy passport, help, help puppy, helpless puppy needs passport, help Marine help helpless puppy—I'm feeling kind of frantic about the whole thing and getting nowhere at the speed of light.

As I'm trying to go to sleep that first night without Lava, all this crap is shooting through my head with the velocity of bullets fired in rapid succession. GO-1A. Vaccinations. Bodies. Rules. Regulations. Reasons. Will it hurt? Then as things get weirder and weirder like they do in the middle of the night, the unauthorized thoughts start rolling in to the tune of "When Johnny Comes Marching Home Again," oo-*rah*, oo-*rah*. So I get up, start the Humvee, and drive across base to the Lava Dogs' building seeing all these weird things and thinking all these weird thoughts like how in the *hell* could someone shoot a dog like that? Orders? *Orders?* Since when do Marines follow orders?

When I get there, it's all dark and everyone's zonked out and I can't see Lava anywhere.

"Hey, little guy," I whisper, expecting him to leap into my arms with tail-pounding joy.

Instead I hear this tiny growl, Lava's warning that he's about to kick my ass, and then see this wienie shadow rush toward me with tail erect and fur on end screaming *roo-roo-roo-roooooo*.

Bodies shoot up on every cot.

"Hey, hey, hey, it's me . . ."

"Who the *hell* is me?" someone grumbles as I hear the click of several rifles being readied for some action.

I bend down and pick Lava up. "Shh, shh. It's me. Just me."

The bodies plop back down on their cots. Several pound pillows back into place; several Marines use my name—and God's—in vain.

"Hey, hey, calm down," I tell Lava, who's quivering with delight over what he's done and with what he's found. I sit there for a while in the dark scratching his little ears until he finally calms down and curls up asleep in my lap.

Am I insane?

I am a lieutenant colonel in the United States Marine Corps. I am an officer in a brotherhood that always goes in first, and that pretty much sums it up right there. We're brave to the point of insanity, so being a Marine takes a certain kind of mind-set to begin with.

Which means you don't always follow orders.

The common belief is that you go in a boy and come out a man, like they have this magical ability to change who you *are*, but the truth of the matter is, we were insane going in and insane coming out, only now we sing this anthem and know cool martial arts.

Insane isn't the right word exactly. None of us really believes Marines guard the streets of Heaven, but how sane is it to *want* to go in first? I can sit aside from this and in a cool, calculated, scientific manner look at it for what it is: not insanity, but a primitive gene that requires some of us to be the fittest and the bravest and the best-est there is, and then the public relations brass throws in the word *proud-est* so we don't feel like cavemen on caffeine.

It's not because we didn't belong or didn't like team sports, and it's not because we couldn't afford college or were manipulated by recruiters or dumped by some chick and then had to prove a point. Those guys joined the army. We didn't have rotten childhoods, we didn't hate math, we didn't bully skinny kids on the playground and didn't start fires in the garage.

And it's not like we joined up without thinking about it, or like once we got in they didn't give us time to think about it. Believe me, sleep deprivation, food rationing, and sit-ups make you think a whole hell of a lot about it. We weren't coerced. We weren't brainwashed. Our souls weren't plundered.

We just can't help it.

We aren't cut out for anything else. We were Marines going in and Marines coming out. We don't *want* to take orders.

And you want to know something? I don't care anymore. I used to, when I first joined up. I worried about my parents' objections, my college buddies' sneers, being called a "jarhead" for the rest of my adult life. But hell if I could help it. The minute I signed on the dotted line, I had this sort of out-of-body party that hasn't been matched since.

Oo-rah.

Listening to these guys snore around me, I really like what I am—a Marine. I like being strong. I like being brave. I like going in first. I *want* to go in first, and I'll be damned if I'm going to let anyone shoot my puppy.

CHAPTER TEN

December 2004
Rancho Santa Fe, California

JOHN VAN ZANTE was having trouble concentrating on the conference call. It was an important one, meant to spawn ideas for an upcoming pet adoption drive for the Helen Woodward Animal Center,
but the new mission kept bullying his concentration.

The new mission was when John's boss, Michael Arms, had told
him about a Marine who needed help getting a puppy out of Iraq.
Apparently a series of e-mails sent out by some lieutenant colonel
in Fallujah wound their way through friends and friends of friends
to Michael Arms, who, as a former Marine in Vietnam and now
the president of the Helen Woodward Animal Center, didn't have a
choice about whether he'd help out or not. The mission of the center—"people helping animals and animals helping people"—and the
mission of the Marines, former or otherwise, wouldn't allow it.

"Are you going to help?" John had asked.

"Of course *we'll* help," Arms said. "Will you take care of it?"

John shook his head. Help? *His* help? He didn't know how much
help he could offer from Rancho Santa Fe. The town was located
just outside San Diego, a major military town, and while talk of the
war infused almost every conversation, this story brought it closer to

home than he was used to. Now when he heard the stories coming out of Iraq, they projected all sorts of images into his head that he knew were ridiculous but couldn't turn off: little puppy squished to death in Marine's backpack; little puppy run over by a tank; little puppy beheaded by insurgents.

What in the heck possessed a three-tour, tough-guy Marine to try to save a little puppy in the middle of a war, anyway? And why was he, an easygoing public relations guy, now being looked to for help? He wasn't a soldier. He didn't know anything about Iraq.

While the center offered a variety of programs supporting the bond between humans and animals, including a Pet Encounter Therapy Program, an adoption center, a therapeutic riding program, and an equine hospital, John wasn't so sure they were equipped to rescue a puppy from Iraq.

The center focused on bringing knowledge, compassion, and respect to all living things. Lofty ideals, sure, but put into actual practice. The Pet Encounter Therapy, for instance, brought animals—dogs, rabbits, birds—to homes for abused children, hospitals, psychiatric facilities, and senior centers, where residents held and caressed the animals until their blood pressure lowered or their hyperactivity waned or their desire to crawl in a hole and die went away for a few precious hours.

But the center surely didn't have time to focus on one little puppy in Iraq.

Then again, it probably didn't have time *not* to.

The only reason John had taken this job in the first place was because there wasn't enough time to do everything that needed to be done. Years earlier he had shaken hands with mortality after learning that his brother had a stroke and his sister had cancer. He'd decided that while his career in commercial broadcasting paid the bills, it didn't promise great poetics on his tombstone. At least this job gave him a reason to take up oxygen. At least it gave him time to do something that meant something. At least it allowed him to save some people and animals from horrible lives and deaths, but the problem was, saving only some made it harder not to save them all.

And now, since Arms had ordered the go-ahead on helping this Marine and his puppy, John hadn't thought about much else. He read news stories about the war with a new sense of urgency. He studied maps, he investigated export laws, he made phone calls and wrote letters to anyone he thought could help, including California's senators.

The puppy was found abandoned during a house by house search in Fallujah. A Marine Lt. Col. from La Jolla, CA, fell in love with the puppy. We've been working to try to get the puppy transported to the United States . . .

Regardless of party affiliation, we firmly believe that it shows that the United States and our military personnel continue to hold respect for all life. Is there anything more innocent than a puppy?

Any help or direction you can provide will be greatly appreciated . . . time is of the essence.

○

Today's conference call included John, his boss, and several executives and public relations people from the Iams pet food company, who were co-sponsoring the Home 4 the Holidays event—the world's biggest pet adoption drive and the center's most important adoption event of the year.

As the center's PR manager, John played an instrumental role in Home 4 the Holidays. The theory of the event was that more families brought pets into their homes during the holidays than at any other time of year, so Iams, the center, and eighteen hundred animal shelters across the world marketed the idea with: "What greater gift can there be than to save the life of an orphan?"

John knew there was no greater gift than to be useful, but convincing people who use well-trained purebred dogs as status symbols to adopt untrained ill-bred mutts was about as easy as convincing lemmings to fight for independence. It was his toughest project of the year, and he *had* to concentrate.

"John?"

He straightened in his chair as he recognized Mike Arms's voice on the other end of the phone.

"Hmm? Yes?"

"Why don't you tell these folks the story about the puppy in Iraq."

Even now, in the middle of the brainstorming session, nine-tenths of John's mind remained burrowed in Fallujah.

"John?"

"Yes?"

"The story about the puppy?"

He had no choice. He launched into the story—". . . and he finds this puppy . . . horrible fighting . . . can't keep pets . . ."—sure that no one in on this conference call would care. He didn't even pause to catch his breath, just sped through the events as fast as he could to get the whole thing over with.

"You can understand why there's an order banning pets, because the Marines are supposed to be concentrating on one thing and one thing only, and I mean we understand why there are rules about this, and I know we need to focus on this pet adoption project, but, but you should read the e-mails, like, I can't imagine what is going on around them over there, and here's a man who was one of our neighbors who is in the middle of a war zone and discovered a life that needed saving and I mean, no matter how you feel about the war, in the middle of this, this horrible battle in Fallujah . . ."

He paused and caught his breath.

". . . life still matters."

When he finished, John sat back in his chair and searched for air.

CHAPTER ELEVEN

December 2004
Camp Fallujah

ONCE I DECIDE to save Lava, it becomes an unprogrammable mission I don't have the smarts to reassign or the guts to walk away from. Only problem is, the enemy doesn't hide out in abandoned buildings whispering *Jihad*; it hangs on the wall of the command center and ticks.

I have forty-eight hours before I leave for Balad, which means I have exactly 2,880 minutes to get approval from brass to transport a puppy on a military flight with Buck, find a veterinarian who will give Lava vaccinations, and then find a way to get Lava to the vet and back in one piece.

I've been exchanging e-mails with this guy named John Van Zante who works for an outfit called the Helen Woodward Animal Center in Rancho Santa Fe. He seems like a nice enough guy and claims the center will try to help Lava and me out. Why? I don't know and don't have time to ask.

During the next two days I grab a computer wherever I can, either in one of the offices or in the command center—a huge, high-ceilinged room with dimmed lights and projectors that are on all the time, showing where our troops are by displaying images from the unmanned drones flying around Fallujah. There's also this big clock on the wall.

○

The Command Center: John Van Zante e-mails me that Iams pet food company wants to help me in any way it can. John and Iams's external relations manager, Kris Parlett, are contacting everyone they can think of—including the entire California congressional delegation—to find the name of an Iraqi veterinarian for me. "We're doing everything we can to bring your puppy home," John writes.

○

The Officers' Building: I shove some gear around, pretending I'm packing. Cammies: check. Ammo: check. Socks: check.

I look at my watch. If I run at my best speed, I can get across base, see Lava, and be back at the computer within thirty minutes. Soap: check. Razor: check. More ammo: check.

But I can't spare thirty minutes just to feed the emotional weakness that's surfaced in my life. Three pictures of Lava: check, check, check.

○

The Command Center: John Van Zante and Kris Parlett have found an Iraqi veterinarian. Corks unpop in my head. This vet, Dr. Farah Murrani, is well known for helping stray animals. She worked with US military in Baghdad when the city's zoo was bombed and, with the help of the US Army, formed the Iraqi Society for Animal Welfare in January 2004.

At that point Dr. Murrani was increasingly seen as a pro-US collaborator, and when two of her friends who acted as interpreters for the United States were shot and killed, she fled Iraq for the United States. She's willing to help, according to the e-mail forwarded to me:

This is Dr. Farah Murrani from Iraqi Society for Animal Welfare in Baghdad, I got the e-mail you sent to Cheyenne Mountain Zoo. If the puppy owner in Baghdad can take the puppy to ISAW, they will be able to provide all the needs including a health certificate. ISAW is based in: Baghdad, Zawra Park, across the road from Baghdad Zoo. Let them contact me for any questions on my e-mail address.

A "milk run" is leaving Camp Fallujah for Baghdad tomorrow, and while theoretically I could get Lava on the convoy and be back in time to get him to Buck, milk runs to Baghdad are susceptible to all kinds of problems—hit and runs, mostly—and coordinating the trips doesn't always go as planned. Besides, they'd have to hide Lava in one of the vehicles, and knowing him he'd make sure every commanding officer in the convoy know he was there ready to protect against all enemies.

If we can get Lava to Baghdad and if he gets his vaccinations and if he gets backs in time to get on Buck's flight, John Van Zante says Iams will pay all the expenses.

It's a long, unfocused shot, but with time running out, it's the only shot I have.

○

The Command Center:

Dr. Murrani, I am the Marine trying to get the puppy to a vet in Baghdad. I might have an opportunity to do so tomorrow (Wednesday) here in Iraq. I'd have to have them meet me somewhere in the International Zone, and would have to leave the puppy in their care for a month or so—I'll gladly pay any expenses (medical care, food, etc) and make a donation to your clinic or the Baghdad Zoo as a token of my appreciation—until I can pick it up again after my next assignment. If this is suitable, please let me know, and please provide me with the e-mail

-address of the person I should contact in the morning. Thank you in advance for your assistance. All the Marines have become very fond of Lava, as we are calling him, and want him to have the best possible care.

○

The Command Center: No response yet from Dr. Murrani.

○

The Command Center: No response yet from Dr. Murrani.

○

The Command Center: No response yet from Dr. Murrani.

○

The Lava Dogs' Building: Lava pees when I walk into the room where he's stashed. He pees now whenever I see him. I think it's because I usually wake him up, like tonight, and he's just happy to see me, but one of the guys says it's a dog's sign of submission, which bothers me for reasons I don't have time to pin down.

○

The Command Center: No response yet from Dr. Murrani.

○

The Command Center: No response yet from Dr. Murrani.

○

The Command Center: She has to contact me. She *has* to. I have 4.2 hours left before I report to the helicopter landing pad, but all I can think about is getting over to the Lava Dogs' building to see the little guy one more time. There isn't any more time, though. I let it escape, and now all I have to show for myself is poorly packed gear and a sick feeling down in my gut.

The Lava Dogs have promised to keep him as long as they can, but he's such a little warrior, they'll have trouble keeping him quiet when the wrong people are around. He senses enemies right away, and even though you beg him to shut up, try to give him a treat, tell him the person he's *rooing* at is a commander who can have him shot, which will hurt, hurt a lot, he gets so worked up, it doesn't get through.

○

The landing zone: We leave for Balad at night to avoid detection. But the chopper—a ninety-nine-foot-long Stallion that can travel 180 miles per hour and carry sixteen tons of cargo—makes this *whomp whomp whomp* so heavy and loud that anyone within ten miles will hear you coming. If you're smart and don't want to collect disability pay for hearing loss the rest of your life, you wear earplugs.

As the whomping starts overhead, everyone on board moves around doing things, shifting things, preparing for things. Me, I sit here in the open door and see Lava peeing. A sign of submission. Jeez. I want him to be loyal, but I don't want him to be submissive to anyone. I want him to survive.

The chopper lifts off. We'll be flying low. The lights of Camp Fallujah disappear.

PART II

"And to dust you shall return."

Genesis 3:19

CHAPTER TWELVE

May 2005
Baghdad

DAVID MACK LOOKED over the paperwork again. It couldn't be legitimate. But Ken Licklider had already given the go-ahead and Brad Ridenour was already on his way in from Kirkurk, so it would have to do.

David had been Ken's overseas manager in Afghanistan and Iraq for the past three years, which meant he knew how to engineer bridges across the rules as well as anyone. Not that there were many rules to follow around here, which made you crazy sometimes, because a lot of rules got made up along the way, like how much in "fees" you had to pay for certain paperwork, for instance, so you never knew what to expect. You never thought you wanted to follow the rules until there weren't any to follow.

It wasn't that the Coalition Provisional Authority didn't challenge the country with rules; it just hadn't developed the biceps to enforce them. With the military busy hunting down insurgents and employing every available noninsurgent Iraqi male to do so, too, it was left to the private security companies like Triple Canopy Security to do most of the police work. Only they had other jobs to do. They were hired to protect, not enforce.

On top of that, there were two sets of rules you had to know about: those in Baghdad's Red Zone and those in the Green Zone.

In the Red Zone the rules were simple — (1) Move fast; (2) Stay alive — and were enforced by whoever possessed the best pyrotechnic talents or drove the fastest armored vehicles.

In the Green Zone, where David stayed at the Triple Canopy compound, the rules took on a more ceremonious air. They had to, because that's where the center of the universe most recently planted its flag.

The Green Zone of Baghdad — surrounded by reinforced, blast-proof concrete slabs, coils of barbed wire, earthen berms, chain-link fences, and dozens of armed checkpoints, and guarded by helicopters, Abrams tanks, armored Humvees, Bradley Fighting Vehicles, and foot patrols — was the ultimate gated community. It was a well-protected bubble, a private club that admitted only the new Iraqi elite, including members of the vague ruling authority, coalition partners of one kind or another, and employees of major US consulting companies.

Located in the center of the city, the Green Zone consisted of much former glamour — Saddam Hussein's former presidential palaces, villas built for former royal family members, stately homes of former Ba'ath party members, former convention centers, former museums, former parks, former parade routes, and former pens for Saddam Hussein's man-eating lions. There was taxi service within its boundaries, a hospital, barbershops, and two Chinese restaurants run by Iraqis.

If you weren't lucky enough to get lodging in one of the palaces, you usually stayed in a single-wide trailer surrounded by sandbags. But that was still better than living in the Red Zone, because at least in the Green Zone, everyone spoke English and had access to CNN, so you knew what was going on outside the perimeter.

The Triple Canopy complex David Mack stayed in was a self-contained, walled compound within the self-contained, walled

Green Zone. It had its own guard towers inhabited day and night by a foreign security force that watched over the individual housing units, the dining hall, the laundry, the gym, the kennels, and the shipping containers full of ammunition. If you had to stay in Baghdad, this was the place to be.

But things were still dangerous. Mortars came across the Green Zone wall all the time, so the rules, the ones that existed anyway, went with the flow.

There was an e-mail making the rounds of private contractors that kind of summed things up:

> **You've Been in Iraq Too Long If . . .**
> *You start to think, It's not so bad here.*
> *You don't jump when a door slams or someone drops something.*
> *A Glock or 9mm on a lady's hip is considered sexy.*
> *Mortars and rocket sounds are okay compared with vehicle bombs.*
> *You can measure distances based on explosive sounds.*
> *You know the difference between "incoming" and "outgoing."*
> *Sitting around with your co-workers talking about different ways to be*
> *   killed is considered "watercooler talk."*
> *Bullet holes in cars are no longer alarming.*
> *Driving on the sidewalk is normal.*
> *Driving on the wrong side of a divided four-lane street is considered*
> *   normal.*
> *Hit-and-run fender benders are treated as mere warnings.*
> *You have your own roll of toilet paper stashed in your car.*
> *You think the bullet holes in the roof of your trailer are just another*
> *   form of ventilation.*

So whether the paperwork in David Mack's hands was legitimate or not was really a matter of interpretation. Only there were lots of different interpreters around these days, and this one worried him.

CHAPTER THIRTEEN

January 2005
Balad

BALAD ISN'T LIKE a super-secret mission or anything, but the group I work with—Task Force 6-26—is a special operations unit that pursues high-value individuals like Abu Musab al-Zarqawi. We also work with Iraqi prisoners whom we suspect know the most important stuff, stuff that could help break the back of the insurgency, but who don't want to tell us what they know.

I have great accommodations, including a trailer with my own room, a real bed, a refrigerator, a closet, and a wall locker. There is a bathroom with a real sit-down, flushable toilet, a sink, and a shower. We have a gym that back home would have cost a five-hundred-dollar initiation fee and fifty bucks a month to join, plasma TVs in our command center, and a full PX complete with a Burger King.

It might have been a great mission except this one thing that keeps pecking away at me, this thing I have to do that I don't want to do.

From the minute I get to Balad, I keep hoping that something will just happen magically behind my back to solve everything concerning Lava. He's still safe with the Lava Dogs back at Camp Fallujah, but when I see John Van Zante's e-mail, which looks like a note of encouragement but smells suspiciously like a note of condolence, I remember that nothing magical has occurred in Iraq since God took one of Adam's ribs.

Iams will help in any way they can. If there are any supplies that you need, please let me know. If you would like puppy food, please tell us where it can be shipped. I will mention that Iams attempted a large shipment to an Iraqi port last year. I was told that it was returned because Iams and Eukanuba dog food contains real animal products which are great for your puppy, but I was told there was an objection on the part of the Iraqi workers who were assigned to unload the food.

But we're standing by to get your puppy home to Rancho Santa Fe once he reaches the USA.

After reading between the lines, I do what I dread doing. I write to Anne Garrels. She's been back in the States for less than thirty days but is scheduled to return to Baghdad for the elections later this month. I hate writing to her, because she was fried when she left Fallujah, but I do it anyway and ask her if she can keep Lava in Baghdad with her when she returns, just until I figure something out.

"Just for a little while," I promise.

○

In the meantime, I finally receive an e-mail from Dr. Murrani after several weeks of waiting.

Dear Sir, I'm so sorry but I only got to see you msg. today, I was so busy that I haven't checked my box. I don't know if this is still helpful or not . . .

Dr. Murrani says that if I can get Lava to Baghdad, the people running the ISAW can give him vaccinations. The problem is, the clinic isn't in the protected Green Zone, which means I'll have a hell of a time finding someone to take him there, and even if I can, she informs me that Lava has to be at least four months old to get his rabies shot, and I figure him to be two months or less.

"Do you know anyone in Baghdad who might watch him for a little while?" I write back. "I'm at a real loss because it would be terrible if we have to put him out of the base on his own. He's really too young—and now too dependent—to survive on his own."

Dr. Murrani says she'll contact some friends living in the Green Zone and see if they'll take Lava in. "I can't really guarantee anything," she writes, "but I will try."

Then I hear from Anne, who promises to try to keep Lava in Baghdad for a few weeks until after the elections, when she'll leave for Cairo. Lava has a few more weeks of borrowed time.

I hear that traps have been set at Camp Fallujah to catch stray dogs and that the Lava Dogs' executive officer has found out about Lava and started honking about GO 1-A in a very loud way.

I learn that the guys sneak him over to the personal security detachment, which provides security for the commanding general at Camp Fallujah. I hiss at the computer screen when I read that message.

The commanding general's personal security detachment? They're the guys who follow all the rules, because they're protecting the most important person on campus whose job it is to make the rules in the first place. What in the hell are they *thinking*?

CHAPTER FOURTEEN

January 2005
Camp Fallujah

TURNS OUT, THE Lava Dogs are thinking hard to find the last place on camp anyone would look for contraband and about the last person anyone would suspect of harboring it. They determined that Sergeant Matt Hammond with the personal security detachment for the commanding general fit the bill.

Matt Hammond is a good Marine, dedicated beyond belief, a patriotic kind of guy who grew up an army brat and worshiped the Marines from the time he was a kid, who always knew he'd sign up, who to this day says the Marines were his childhood heroes, which makes the rest of us feel like imposters, because we grew up worshiping the Beaver's big brother and Cap'n Crunch.

This is how loyal Matt Hammond is:

He's in Fallujah, right? Patrolling or whatever, and it's bad there now, right? Like, there's no electricity, water, or sewage in the city, and because dead bodies rot everywhere—under the rubble, inside the houses, out on the streets—the air is as alien as gas on another planet. In all at least twelve hundred insurgents and an unknown number of noncombatants have been killed and forty-four Marines have already been processed through the Mortuary Affairs Unit at the camp.

Matt gets wounded one night in an alley, and the guys load him into a Humvee and rush to a nearby aid station. But on the way a grenade hits the Humvee and the door's locking mechanism dislodges, sending Matt out onto the street. They have to turn around to pick him up, and while they're looking for him in the dark, another firefight erupts. Matt is conscious during all of this, lying there on the street, and to hear him tell the rest of the story almost kills your throttle:

"I didn't know what happened. They came back for me, but it was so dark, they couldn't see me and there was another firefight. I remember I couldn't breathe and I was trying to crawl toward them. All I remember after that is hearing them yell, 'We found him! We found him!'

"After that, I was transported to a hospital in Baghdad, but when they told me I would have to go to a hospital in Germany, I snuck out and called my buddies back at Camp Fallujah and told them I didn't want to leave. I told them to come and get me.

"I was on a lot of morphine, and one day I was just lying in bed in the hospital half asleep and I hear this voice that sounds like the commanding general. I could hear him saying, 'Put on your boots. You've got a war to fight.' I thought I was dreaming but it *was* him. He'd come to Baghdad to take me back."

When the chopper landed at Camp Fallujah later that day, Matt's team sat in Humvees waiting for him in the landing area.

"It felt like I'd just hit a grand slam and was coming into home base with everyone there waiting to cheer me on."

Matt is, like, dedicated. Loyal as a cliché. And he loves dogs.

So while he's recouping at the camp in his team's building and the Lava Dogs sneak the puppy to him, he looks at it like a mission. See, he can't stand the fact that the guys in his team are going out to work every day while he's stuck in the building trying to learn how to walk again, so taking care of Lava gives him something to *do*.

Only he learns right away what a little beast Lava is and starts wondering if the puppy has coyote blood in him or something. He's smaller than a sandbag but acts like a wild animal. That's a direct quote: ". . . acts like a wild animal."

Lava chews on anything that belongs to anybody—pillows, blankets, clothes, plastic gun butts—and when he discovers the guy's rubber shower shoes, he goes on his own little search-and-destroy mission. Then he singles out one Marine's boots and pees on them—and only them—night after night. And then there's his compulsive need to protect the guys from noise and shadow, any noise or shadow, and his incessant *roo-rooing* starts getting on their combat-sawed nerves.

Matt finally decides that in order to save his life, especially from the Marine with the squishy boots, he'd better get Lava his own barracks. So he commandeers the navy Seabees on base to build Lava a little plywood hooch, which they hide in back of the building.

And eventually Matt and Lava fall into a nice little routine. In the mornings, Matt and Lava water the makeshift garden grown from seeds Matt's mom sent from Arizona. Then they sit behind the building and play with toys sent by the team's family members back home when they heard they had a puppy. Then they amble down to a bombed-out sewer at the edge of the camp to feed a litter of puppies the guys found one day.

But everyone knows it's just a matter of time before the wrong people find out about Lava. For one thing, he's growing bigger and getting louder every day. For another, a week or so after Matt starts feeding the stray puppies, someone following orders covers the sewer with the puppies in it over with dirt.

CHAPTER FIFTEEN

January 2005
The Syrian Border

BY THE TIME the elections are one week away, Annie is in flight to Baghdad, Lava is still at Camp Fallujah, and I'm at the Syrian border. I'm back to babysitting Iraqi soldiers, who in this part of the country call themselves the Desert Wolves.

I'm worried about Lava, whom I haven't seen in more than a month. I'm also worried about Matt and his guys, who are arranging a special convoy they're calling a "chow run" to get him to Baghdad. Marines are prime targets these days, and the insurgents and everyone related to them hate our guts for what we did in Fallujah. But I'm most worried about Anne, who's going to have to pick him up somewhere in the city the Ref seems to be pissing on these days.

The election is scheduled for January 30; Iraqis will vote for a national assembly to write a new constitution and for council members to represent each of the eighteen provinces in the country. The problem is that the Shiites and ethnic Kurds make up about 80 percent of the country's population and are expected to win by a landslide, and because Sunnis, who know they will lose, are threatening to boycott the election in protest of our destruction of Fallujah, so civil war is rolling in like an enemy tank so poorly oiled you can hear it coming a mile away.

I'm all keyed up about Lava going to Baghdad, because it's, like, *tense* there right now. The country hasn't seen open voting since before the reign of Saddam Hussein. For Iraqis starved of political power, the ballot represents an all-you-can-eat buffet, and the diners are hungry, and a lot of them have guns.

I mean, get this. A total of 196 political parties and 33 coalitions representing more than 18,900 candidates rush to get on the ballot. The ballot provides voters a heaping helping of hastily formed parties such as the United Iraqi Coalition, the Iraqi Islamic Party, and the Constitutional Monarchy Movement, each providing lists of candidates, including "the Iraqi List," "the Security and Stability List," and "the Security and Justice List."

The election authorities try to keep order—you can't be funded by a militia, for example—and each registrant has to provide a logo or symbol so illiterate voters can identify them. When logos of Kalashnikov rifles, mass graves, and Korans with halos around them start showing up, everyone knows it's going to get messy.

But as quickly as candidates register, they receive death threats or, as in the case of at least ten of them, well-placed bullets to the head. Candidates are afraid to leave their homes, and unless a party has its own militia, its people can't run for office and stay alive at the same time. Campaigning, therefore, is done Iraqi-style: Candidates hire people to run out on the streets, post a few signs, and then run back inside before they're seen.

Slogans on the signs are straightforward and simple: FREE HOMELAND—HAPPY PEOPLE! or WE WILL RESTORE ELECTRICITY! A few candidates, including interim prime minister Iyad Allawi, pay for television airtime: "We will strive to reduce unemployment by using oil investments to create 250,000 new jobs in the public and private sectors . . ." But even the prime minister isn't immune from threats. Soon after his television ad is aired, an al-Qaeda affiliate posts a videotape on the Internet showing a candidate from Allawi's party being murdered. The tape includes a warning to the prime minister: "You traitor, wait for the angel of death." So most candidates avoid public appearances and just hide in their homes and pray.

Right before the election, the government, such as it is, plans to close the borders, cut all mobile and satellite phone service, and ban travel between provinces. It also announces that it has stockpiled hospital beds and medical supplies in anticipation of democracy.

So, yeah, I'm worried about Lava and Matt and Anne.

I mean, reading the headlines in the week leading up to the election turns monotonous:

AT LEAST 21 PEOPLE KILLED BY SUICIDE BOMBERS

BAGHDAD GOVERNOR ALI AL-HAYDARI ASSASSINATED

AT LEAST 20 PEOPLE KILLED IN INSURGENT ATTACKS

MILITANTS BEHEAD IRAQI WHO WORKED FOR THE COALITION AND
   KILL AT LEAST FOUR OTHERS

MILITANTS KILL EIGHT IRAQI NATIONAL GUARD SOLDIERS

ELEVEN PEOPLE DIE IN SUICIDE BOMBINGS

AT LEAST 14 PEOPLE KILLED AND 40 WOUNDED BY CAR BOMB NEAR
   SHI'A MUSLIM MOSQUE

BOMB DETONATES NEAR IRAQI PREMIER'S OFFICES

IRAQI JUDGE ASSASSINATED IN BAGHDAD

CAR BOMB AT A PROVINCIAL GOVERNMENT HEADQUARTERS KILLS
   FIVE PEOPLE

20 PEOPLE KILLED IN SERIES OF ATTACKS INVOLVING ROCKETS,
   ROADSIDE EXPLOSIVES, AND SUICIDE CAR BOMBS

After a while it's like reading something from Dr. Seuss: *They behead them in Baghdad, yes they do, so make sure your hotel has a room with a view.*

People stationed or stuck in Baghdad are starting to unravel as all these contractors and civilians and Iraqi soldiers get killed. As for the US forces, we don't fare much better. During the month of January, 641 of our troops are killed or wounded.

This includes thirty-one Lava Dogs who go down in a helicopter during a sandstorm four days before the election.

CHAPTER SIXTEEN

January 2005
The Syrian Border

I CHECK MY e mail one more time before going to bed. When I see Anne's name in the inbox, worry surrenders with hands up to a sense of panic I hadn't felt during even the worst of the fighting in Fallujah.

Earlier in the week the guys at Camp Fallujah created an excuse to convoy to Baghdad where they're supposed to hand Lava over to Anne, but the wait for the exchange—the trip to Baghdad and then the actual handover—turns into this foxhole of hours, because I have no way of knowing what's going on. I could play handball with an undetonated grenade and feel calmer.

One of the guys e-mailed that morning, needing the PIN of my cell so he could call Anne and arrange the drop-off. I haven't heard anything since, so I don't know if he got hold of Anne or if Anne answered the call or if the guys got off base or if the convoy made it to Baghdad or if Anne got into the Green Zone or if the Marines, Anne, and Lava are even still alive.

I know better. I know I know better. My trust in my fellow Marines is bulletproof. Whether directing an E2C Hawkeye onto a carrier or covering my back in a Fallujah alley, I know they'll perform as trained. But rescuing Lava is something different. Waiting like this requires an alien faith. If Lava jumps out of the Humvee on the way to Baghdad, will they jump out, too, and go after him? If an officer discovers the puppy in the convoy and orders him shot, will they do it? If they can't get off base in Baghdad, if they can't find Annie, if they get a call from home and miss the handoff, will they figure out another way or will they leave him on the streets?

You never ask your men to do anything you won't do yourself. You parachute first, you help clear the way, you count inventory alongside them so they trust you. But would I have done any of those things for anyone else's puppy if he'd asked me to? To this day I'm not sure.

I should have just walked away from Lava the day I left Fallujah. Sure, it would have been tough, but guilt only annoys you if you pay attention to it, like a crook in your neck, and then I wouldn't have had all these nights of worry about who was caring for Lava, what would happen if the wrong people discovered him, and how they would kill him if they found him. I wouldn't have had to spend time playing with him and feeding him and finding a way to get him vaccinations and food from the military working dog handlers.

But all the things I did for him, I did for myself. They helped me forget all the crap over here, and I spend all day and night waiting to hear anything, anything at all, even that he hasn't made it.

Now Anne's e-mail sits before me with the potential of an IED.

You normally couldn't worry like this, about how expensive life was here, about how you budgeted each breath and horded each heartbeat because it might be the last. Thinking about it is unauthorized, off limits, quarantined until notice, because if you obsess about death or search for stronger gods or stare too long at the navel of your own future, you lose focus and get shot in the head.

You have to be tougher than this, stronger than this, smarter than this. But when I finally work up the courage to open Anne's e-mail, I break down and cry.

CHAPTER SEVENTEEN

January 2005
Baghdad

ANNE ALWAYS TOLD me that most Americans don't understand how two different countries exist within the boundaries of Baghdad. Even the Marines from Camp Fallujah who contacted her about handing Lava over didn't quite get it. Her e-mail explains all of it, but what really gets me is how it ends.

Anne stays in a compound in the city's Red Zone. It's a far cry from the hotel she reported from in 2003, when she was one of only sixteen American journalists who stayed in Baghdad during the initial invasion of Iraq by US and British forces. While during the siege she faced constant censorship from the Iraqis under Saddam Hussein—she reported from her hotel room naked in case the Iraqi police barged in—at least she could go out on the streets and buy kebabs for lunch.

But now, two years after the first onslaught of Operation Iraqi Freedom, two distinct zones divide Baghdad—the heavily guarded Green Zone, where if clothed in a flak jacket you can still safely buy kebabs on the street, and the unprotected Red Zone, where captive Americans bring twenty-five thousand dollars apiece and flak jackets only weigh you down when you need to run.

At first the Fallujah Marines want Anne to meet them at the air-port to pick Lava up, but that's too dangerous, because she doesn't have an armored car in which to travel the strip of highway between Baghdad and the airport known as "IED Alley." When the Marines finally comprehend the impracticality of that plan, they think it's simply a matter of meeting her somewhere in the Green Zone. But Anne lives in the Red Zone, which is an area of free-for-all violence consisting of bombed-out schools, bombed-out restaurants, and bombed-out office buildings that receive no clean water and only a few hours of electricity on good days. She *wants* to be there, in the real Iraq.

The Red Zone is governed for the most part by insurgents and private security contractors—hired protection specialists who, un-supervised by military law, drive down sidewalks in armored SUVs waving automatic weapons to clear their way.

No one leaves the Green Zone without an armed convoy. No one enters the Green Zone without credentials, and even those with the credentials have to pass through several checkpoints of heavy metal gates, coiled concertina wire, metal road spikes, blast barriers, and sandbagged isolation bays used for searches.

While some consider Fallujah the most dangerous place on earth, others believe waiting in line to pass into Baghdad's Green Zone is worse. Stopped vehicles make easy targets for snipers, and car bombs explode here by the dozens, so US and Iraqi guards di-vide incoming traffic into two lanes, one for VIPs that moves fairly quickly and one for everyone else. The process of getting in is so time consuming that in January, Iraq's minister of state resigned in anger over how he was treated when he tried to enter the Green Zone for a cabinet meeting.

In order to get into the Green Zone to pick up Lava, Anne has to wait in line with everyone else. Once inside, she can't just travel wherever she wants. No one but the Marines can do that, so when they suggest meeting at one of the military bases on the inside, she informs them that she can't go anywhere in the Green Zone but the former convention center.

The handoff grows even more complicated when the Fallujah Marines can't find the convention center. They try calling Anne by cell, but the city's only service, provided by Iraqna, has its daily four-hour siesta at that point. Iraqna, handed an exclusive two-year contract by the Coalition Provisional Authority, blames its blackouts on chaos—no fuel, no electricity, no banking system, no generators, no landlines—and sabotage and the US military, which regularly shuts down the network to keep insurgents from communicating with one another and from setting off bombs.

So Anne has to just sit tight and wait until she finally sees the whole group of them wandering around down the street carrying Lava in their arms.

When they finally connect, Matt hands Lava over to Anne. It's kind of an ordeal for him, because, you know, he's a Marine standing in front of a bunch of other Marines who don't want to see one of their own all wimped out over a puppy, only they're all a little wimped out over the puppy, and Anne, who doesn't want to be seen in the company of wimpy Marines, grabs Lava and leaves as fast as she can.

He doesn't have a collar or leash, so Anne has to carry him all the way back to the car. Luckily her Iraqi driver doesn't object. Most Iraqis don't like dogs.

But getting from the Green Zone back to the NPR compound in the Red Zone is no joyride, either; it requires a certain amount of grit and heavy-duty sedatives if available.

If you're fortunate enough to live in the Green Zone, but unfortunate enough to have to go into the Red Zone, you travel the streets escorted either by a military convoy or, more likely, by a private security detail driving custom-built SUVs with steel-plated doors, three-inch bulletproof windows, and machine guns pointing out every available crack. Local traffic swerves out of the way for these guys, even onto the sidewalks or into oncoming traffic in the opposite lane.

Not that there are many rules of the road to obey here in the first place. Traffic lights blink sporadically and there aren't any cops waiting to catch speeders, so drivers run through intersections and speed across sidewalks and generally avoid anything that might contain a bomb, including cars stopped for pedestrians, cars moving slowly through intersections, and cars stalled in the middle of the street.

If you're unfortunate enough to live in the Red Zone and have to actually go somewhere within it, the safest way to travel is as discreetly as possible. Nothing showy. No American flags on the antenna, no SUPPORT OUR TROOPS bumper stickers. Armored sedans are to be avoided because, as William Langewiesche reported in *The Atlantic Monthly*, they "might get you through a short gunfight, but they can kill you too, particularly through the overpressure that results from the explosion of a rocket-propelled grenade that penetrates to the inside." Thin-skinned sedans are the way to go, because while they won't stop bullets, they allow "rocket grenades to pass right through."

And here Annie is, transporting a large puppy who can't keep still and whose face, popping up from one window to another, announces with virtual spotlights and blaring trumpets to every person standing in the streets that an American and her dirty American dog are in the car.

CHAPTER EIGHTEEN

January 2005
The Syrian Border

I DON'T CARE that I haven't cried since I was a kid. When I read Anne's e-mail from Baghdad, not even Patton's presence could keep the tears from coming.

"Just to confirm that Lava is safely with me . . ."

Am I a gutless wimp?

Maybe.

Have I just embarrassed the entire US Marine Corps?

Perhaps.

Do I care?

CHAPTER NINETEEN

February 2005
Baghdad

ANNE'S DAYS IN Baghdad start early. Until 5 am, Lava snuggles up next to her in bed and snores, but at 5 am sharp the security people in the building rotate in and out, which sends Lava diving off the bed, to the door, to the window, and back to the door in a fanatic frenzy of barking.

Back in the States, Anne and her husband live with five dogs, so she understands canine instinct well, but she tells me that never *ever* has she met a dog, especially one as young as Lava, who bounces so wildly back and forth between innocence and sheer ferocity. She thinks maybe it's his gene pool; there are so many stray and feral dogs in Iraq that anything could be governing his DNA. Maybe the bombs did it or maybe his early diet of MREs, but Anne guesses it has something more to do with being raised by homesick Marines.

Lava is a toy version of the well-trained, loyal-hearted, loud-mouthed grunt. He sits on command. He pees outside. He obeys to the point of mechanization, but threaten the safety of his loved ones—especially at five o'clock in the morning—and nothing holds back the *roo-roo-rooing*.

The building, really a compound of small buildings surrounded by a high wall, sits in the Red Zone and houses the NPR crew, other reporters, an Iraqi staff, and the security personnel.

There aren't any cinemas, no restaurants, no trivia nights at the local mosque, so the highlight of everyone's day at the compound is to fawn over Lava's incredible ability to sit.

"Watch *this*," one of them says to the others for the sixth time that evening, then looks down at Lava and raises a hand ever, ever, ever so slightly.

"Sit."

And the intelligent puppy looks up, wags his tail, and *sits*. It's amazing. Everyone, even the Iraqi workers, *oohs* and *aahs* as if encouraging the spiritual progress of the next Dalai Lama.

Anne e-mails me with updates when she can.

"All is well. Lava is happy . . ."

"He's incredibly affectionate. He nips but no more than our Lab puppy back home . . ."

"He sits beautifully . . ."

○

Before the insurgency gained popularity, journalists in Baghdad usually just congregated in the big hotels. After the initial invasion, though, after Saddam Hussein fled and the electricity went out, the reality of being invaded set in, and the big hotels became common targets. Journalists then either left the country or moved into private houses, which were less comfortable but definitely less conspicuous. If your house came under insurgent surveillance, you just moved to another house.

But after the coalition forces invaded Fallujah and casualty reports filtered through the rest of the country, hatred of Americans grew so strong that private houses no longer protected anyone. Now the safest places were compounds like this, usually former motels, with high walls, grilled doors, and, most importantly, hired security with fully loaded automatic weapons.

You didn't go out for anything other than reporting, because journalists made especially functional targets out on the streets, with their deaths reported worldwide. Since the invasion in March two years before, seventy-five journalists and their drivers, interpreters, and guards were killed in Iraq by either insurgents, US forces, or Iraqi troops. In the past year alone thirty journalists had been kidnapped.

Now that the initial election is over, Anne expects the violence to get worse. As she reports on NPR: "Sunday's election was the easy part."

On the day of the election, hundreds of insurgent attacks were reported in Iraq, but now as the country waits for the ballots to be counted — a process that will take several weeks — violence barrels in with mud on its shoes. The Shiite Muslim majority expects big wins, and the Sunni Muslims aren't taking the expected loss very well.

A few days after the election Osama bin Laden's top deputy calls the election "forged" and issues a renewed call for holy war. Al-Qaeda meanwhile promises to continue killing Americans and any Iraqis who help them, and keeps true to its word.

Three days after the election two Marines are killed and twelve Iraqi soldiers are executed. Four days after the election a Marine from Camp Fallujah is killed in action and one Task Force Freedom soldier is killed and another wounded when their convoy is hit with a roadside bomb. Five days after the election two Task Force Danger soldiers get whacked and four others get wounded by an improvised explosive device. Seven days after the election twenty-four Iraqi recruits die from a suicide bomber. Eight days after the election another twenty-one join them.

That same week, Italian journalist Giuliana Sgrena is seized from her vehicle by armed men near Baghdad University where she'd just interviewed refugees from Fallujah.

"It's still tense around here," Anne reports.

○

Anne enlists the help of one of the Iraqis who helps take care of the compound to watch Lava when she goes out during the day. That takes some guts, because she stands a good chance of losing him.

For one thing, most Iraqis hate dogs. They think they're unclean.

For another, there's an intense hatred of any Iraqi who works for Americans. If you're Iraqi and work for Americans, you are *worse* than the Americans. First you receive a written warning addressed on the outside to "Brother of the monkey and the pig." Then, on the inside, it reads something along the lines of,

> *Dear brother of the monkey and the pig:*
>
> *We regret to inform you that unless you repent and return to your God and your Country, you will see a similar fate as that of your fellow brother spies who are rats and the afterbirth of rats. We are sorry for any inconvenience our violence may cause you, your wife, or your children.*
>
> *Sincerely, the Self-Sacrificers*

The next message is less diplomatic:

> *WARNING! WARNING! WARNING! You are the enemy of God and Country. We give you this one last warning before death. Signed, Self-Sacrificers.*

Then they might paint DEATH TO SPIES on your house or leave a dead animal at your door. There's rarely a third message left—and if there is, a homemade bomb is usually attached.

While American deaths are meticulously accounted for by the US government—by the end of that January, several thousand and counting—no credit columns are kept on how many Iraqis, whether insurgents or American-hired civilians, are killed or missing.

So I can only imagine what's going through Sam's mind (I'll call him Sam, because if he's still alive, and I really hope he is, his real name can't ever be associated with what he did) when Anne asks him to keep an eye on the puppy.

"What, *that* wild thing? I'd rather sacrifice an eye."

"Please?"

"No. I do not keep eyes on crazy animals. No."

"Please."

"Why not you ask me to shoot a bullet in my foot instead? Ask me to eat pork. Ask me to jump from airplane . . ."

"*Please.*"

And I can only imagine what goes through Sam's head as Anne drives off to work that first time, leaving Lava at his feet staring up at him with that innocent look he gets when he needs to get it, that ears-forward, head-cocked, *I-didn't-mean-to-chew-up-the-only-porn-magazine-in-the-barrack* look that causes you to bend down and scratch his little ears as you piece the pages back together.

At first Sam is responsible for only two things: feeding Lava and making sure he doesn't destroy the compound. After a few days, though, Anne notices that he's expanding his responsibilities. She'll come home and find Sam giving Lava a bath, or rolling a soccer ball around trying to teach him how to block.

One night she finds Lava pawing at a two-inch-wide men's leather belt hanging around his neck. It's way too big, but when she looks to Sam for answers, he explains that "that dog" needs a collar.

Sam is soon out on the streets of Baghdad in search of food and toys, also improvised in the end, because just about everything in the city is in one of two states: chaos or short supply. The price of meat, fruit, and vegetables has risen by at least a third since the US occupation. Electricity, water, and gasoline are also in short supply because of attacks on Iraq's oil infrastructure by insurgents and because the Coalition Provisional Authority is so corrupt and/or inept, it "lost" at least eight million dollars of its budget within a fourteen-month period.

But Sam goes out on the streets anyway, and one of his most valuable discoveries—found while dodging insurgents, hired mercenaries, and American convoys that warn in block letters DO NOT COME WITHIN 100 METERS OF THIS VEHICLE! DEADLY FORCE WILL BE USED!—is puppy biscuits.

○

In the meantime, Anne reports that as the election results continue to be counted, Sunni clerics claim any winners will be "illegitimate," President George Bush announces in his State of the Union address that it is still "too soon" to withdraw from Iraq, and soldiers with the army's First Cavalry Division stationed in Baghdad are allowed two bottles of beer each during a replay of the Super Bowl.

That same day, claims appear on the Mujahideen Brigade's Web site that the kidnapped Italian journalist Giuliana Sgrena has been executed. Almost immediately another militant group, the Islamic Jihad Organization, states on its Web site that *they* have the journalist and she is not dead yet. As Anne returns from interviews that morning, an American convoy passes her vehicle, which is being driven by an Iraqi, and turns around and then follows her for a while through the streets. They eventually stop the car, concerned that *she* has been abducted.

Anne reports that twenty-one people have been killed by a suicide bomber at an Iraqi army recruiting center. "They are clearly targeting Iraqi Special Forces," she says. And indeed, the *Iraqi Resistance Report* announces that an "Iraqi Resistance car bomb exploded near a truck carrying recruits to a puppet troop base in an unused airport in the western part of Baghdad . . . the blast took place near a recruiting center for the puppet troops and killed at least 21 and wounded about 27 more would-be soldiers serving the USA."

Anne e-mails me at the end of that first week.

"He saved my sanity today. I was just so fed up with this whole place, and the whole job and went over and romped with him for awhile."

And I imagine it is almost as if Lava's presence at the compound allows all humans a temporary exit pass from reality and maneuvers them through various checkpoints into the Land of Make-Believe where puppies romp on plush, green grass and it's a beautiful day in the neighborhood.

CHAPTER TWENTY

February 2005
The Syrian Border

TRYING TO COORDINATE Lava's escape from the Syrian border through
e-mail—getting the vaccinations, arranging for the paperwork, keeping him alive one day to the next—feels like being on the moon trying
to shoot fish in a barrel on earth. But a mission on the Syrian border
and a mission on a distant planet are little different anyway. While a
lot of the country's violence depends on what comes and goes across
the border, the vast stretches of sand and horizon make it feel like a
lunar outpost.

My job here includes providing support to the army officers who
are training the new Iraqi border police—the Desert Wolves—and
to the Marines who man the forward operating base. I travel up and
down the desert checking in on the dozens of forts where the new
Desert Wolves stare out into the desert, fidget with their weapons,
and smoke heavily as they wait for payday and their next vacation.

The Desert Wolves are supposed to patrol the Iraq–Syria border,
which foreign mercenaries, weapons smugglers, and jihadists move
across easier than ants through a chain-link fence. During the past
year, corruption raged here in Iraq's "Wild, Wild West," and the
equivalent of fifty dollars bought anyone a one-way ticket through

the checkpoints. While the Marines tracked and fought the insurgent sympathizers in the desert at night, the former Iraqi border police made extra cash by waving them through in broad daylight.

The new guys, the Desert Wolves, seem on the up-and-up so far, but between the constant threats to their lives and the worsening economic conditions in Iraq, I know it's just a matter of time before the huge amounts of cash coming out of Syria, where many of Saddam Hussein's high-ranking Ba'athist party members now live, tempt the new guys beyond endurance.

I understand the instinct to take what you can when you can, especially when your future is locked so deeply within somebody else's battle plan, but if these guys are going to oversee their country's security and US troops are ever going to pull out, then they have to sprout more discipline out here in this barren, unfertile grit.

And the pressure is on. Just this week General Richard B. Myers, chairman of the Joint Chiefs of Staff, told the Senate Armed Services Committee that the United States won't pull out of Iraq until the country's security forces develop the capacity to police their own country. He then assured the committee that the training process was "moving along."

Likewise, in a visit to Iraq, Defense Secretary Donald Rumsfeld announced that "They [Iraqi security forces] are developing confidence and skill."

In Baghdad the US Army general in charge of training the forces told reporters that while there had been "some setbacks," the training of the new Iraqi police and military forces was gaining "considerable momentum."

But as far as I can see, the only thing gaining considerable momentum is the insurgency's attacks against the Iraqi recruits. Though they've been issued 79,000 pistols, 60,000 assault rifles, 94,000 sets of body armor, 5,900 vehicles, 20,900 radios, 2,400 heavy machine guns, 54,000 Kevlar helmets, and 79 million rounds of ammunition, the new Iraqi forces are being killed faster than Americans. More than thirteen hundred had died since we started training them. During the same week that US commanders extolled their "progress" to the media, twelve Iraqi soldiers died in an ambush near Kirkuk, twelve more were killed in Mosul by a suicide bomber, twenty-one died in an explosion outside an Iraqi Army base in Baghdad, six were killed by a car bomb in Baquba, three were killed and eleven others wounded by gunmen attacking an Iraqi Army convoy, twenty decomposing bodies of Iraqi police and soldiers were found on a road near the town of Suwayrah, six Iraqi National Guardsmen were found dead and dumped on a highway near Mosul, and the Associated Press received a videotape of masked gunmen shooting four Iraqi policemen.

So we make day trips out to the forts where the Desert Wolves just watch the border day and night. We go to make sure they're taking turns on watch, that they have the proper security setup, that the lookout posts are where they're supposed to be, but mainly we just want to make sure they're still alive out there.

The insurgents' methods of targeting the Iraqi troops evolved as the war raged on. Because the insurgency apparently found it increasingly difficult to recruit suicide bombers, remote-controlled IEDs gained importance as the weapon of choice. When the United States counteracted with electronic jammers, the insurgents adapted by reverting to hard-to-jam signals.

Now they've gone back to basics—the hardest to counteract and the simplest of all to use—strapping bombs to unwitting others, including dogs, cows, donkeys, and human beings with Down syndrome.

Usually a dog is picked off the streets, rigged with explosives, and then set loose among potential victims. The bomb is then detonated by remote control. In Ramadi insurgents booby-trapped a donkey and then let it loose near a US-run checkpoint, where the donkey exploded. In Al Mashro police "arrested" a cow wandering down a highway dressed in bombs.

The new method became so popular that the daily Arabic-language newspaper *Al Mada* published an editorial cartoon showing an insurgent trying to give a pep talk to a terrified dog: "It is such a simple task. All you have to do is to put on this explosives belt, repeat the party's slogans, and may Allah have mercy on your father's soul!"

But the insurgents in Iraq held no corner on using animals as weapons during war. That distinction probably belongs to Americans, who through the years have used dogs to deliver messages and supplies through dangerous areas, cats to kill rats in foxholes, birds to indicate chemical weapons, and dolphins and seals to spot sea mines. During World War II the Soviet and US armies reportedly trained "tank dogs" who were taken away from their mothers as soon as they were born and fed only underneath tanks. When the dogs grew older, they were starved, rigged with bombs, and then sent out onto the battlefield to search for the nearest tank, hopefully a German one. Once there, the bombs were detonated.

The beauty of using animals to kill is that they don't know any better. Soldiers, Marines, insurgents all had to be trained to kill, which took up time and resources, whereas donkeys and dogs just wanted someone to pet or feed them. The problem with this method, however, is that it is fairly imprecise. After all, you can't direct a cow to "go up to the corner, turn left, walk north for two blocks, and then moo loudly when you get to the line of guys standing outside the police recruiting station."

So they reverted to something even better—people like nineteen-year-old Amar, who had Down syndrome. According to the *Sydney Morning Herald*, Amar's parents went out to vote and then went to a relative's house for a celebratory party. While they were gone, insurgents kidnapped Amar, strapped a bomb to him, and told him to walk toward a polling site.

At least one eyewitness said that Amar "was so scared when ordered to walk to the searching point, he began to walk back to the terrorists."

In response, they blew him up.

Amar's parents heard the blast from their party, and when word spread that a "mongoli" was the bomber, they raced home to find Amar gone. Amar's cousin told the *Sydney Morning Herald*: "They got neighbors to search and one of them identified Amar's head where it lay on the pavement. His body was broken into pieces. I have heard of them using dead people and donkeys and dogs to hide their bombs, but how could they do this to a boy like Amar?"

I don't care how long you've been in Iraq, that sort of thing kicks your ass to the curb and back.

○

It hits me suddenly, like a slap on the back in a crowded room—a major in the army had gotten puppies out of the country some time back. I can't remember the details, because at the time it was just something I heard about, like you'd hear about someone's wife back home having a baby, a nice story in passing but something you think about for a few minutes and then forget. All I remember now is that someone in the State Department had helped her.

I e-mail the major and explain Lava's story.

"Did you actually get your pooches vaccinated?" I write:

> *More importantly, if I could hook up Anne Garrels with your friend at State, do you think he'd help one more time? It would be such a huge favor to ask, I know, but I'm leaving in less than two months—Annie leaves at the end of this month—and I'm running out of ideas. We've even considered asking the Marine C-130 crews to take him with them.*

I'd have to put him in a kit bag, get on a helo to Al Asad, then give him to them to take home . . .

The problem is that I still don't have permission to transport Lava on a military plane, and it doesn't look like I'm going to. In addition, Lava still doesn't have his vaccinations or paperwork and I haven't heard back from Dr. Murrani.

Anyway, if you think you could ask your friend to help once more, I'd appreciate it tremendously.

I'm banking on the fact that the major has been in Iraq for a while and hopefully understands the need for mutual rowing.

She does. She writes back immediately telling me first that she heard a car bomb went off in front of the ISAW in Baghdad, which is probably why I haven't heard back from Dr. Murrani yet; she likely has other issues to deal with.

I got the dogs vaccinated by a military vet. He was very paranoid about it though, and had me meet him in a parking lot in civilian clothes to hand off the records.

[My friend] at State Department claimed [the puppies] as his and had them shipped to Kuwait. From there, Bonnie Buckley at Military Mascots had a very nice lady pick them up and ship them to Atlanta via Amsterdam.

I found the key is to get an Iraqi vet to get them all the shots — rabies most importantly, or get a friend to convoy them to Kuwait and get one of Bonnie's contacts to help from there.

So I Google "Military Mascots" and find out it's a group of volunteers who help service members get their pets out of Iraq and to the United States. It's perfect. It seems like all I'll have to do is contact them and make sure Lava gets his vaccinations and paperwork.

That and get Lava from Baghdad to Kuwait.

CHAPTER TWENTY-ONE

February 2005
Massachusetts

THE MARINE'S LETTER to Bonnie Buckley wasn't that much different from the dozens and dozens of others she'd received during the past two years. At least it wasn't another hate letter accusing her of being a threat to national security. For every e-mail she got requesting help with a mascot, she received another accusing her of aiding and abetting Iraqi spies or bringing foreign diseases into the country: "Foreign dogs carry the plague!"

Bonnie also received messages suggesting she find more worthwhile causes to support, even though she couldn't imagine a better way to spend her time. And besides, this wasn't about saving homeless dogs and cats in a foreign country; as a former animal control officer, Bonnie knew there were plenty of those in the United States already, millions and millions of them. Rather, Military Mascots, the volunteer group she ran from her home in Massachusetts, was about supporting the troops in Iraq and Afghanistan by supplying a patriotic missing link.

She'd created the group in 2003 when she heard about a soldier who'd found a puppy in an oil field in Iraq and wanted to bring him home. She helped raise twelve hundred dollars and since then hadn't stopped helping. She now had nine ports of entry at her disposal along with military parents and spouses, active and retired military members, civilians, and veterinarians across the world organizing everything from flight arrangements to vaccinations to border crossings to help get the animals to the States.

At first Bonnie had no clue how to cut through the international red tape to get an animal across the border. But the never-ending stream of requests drove her to make repeated phone calls to foreign embassies, spend enormous amounts of time on the Internet, and devote even more time to networking with animal rescue organizations, military personnel, and veterinarians across the world.

The organization now ran an underground railroad from Iraq and Afghanistan through Jordan and Kuwait. "Nothing illegal," she would tell anyone who wondered, though some things hovered near the edge. Like, she used to try to smuggle dogs out on military flights by having them drugged, so they wouldn't be noticed. But she didn't do that anymore. Everything was on the up-and-up, all the paperwork, everything.

While she knew that in every war there were cases of service members finding and adopting pets in foreign lands, she sensed that those now deployed in the Middle East were especially in need of the morale boost the animals seemed to give. She received so many pleas for help.

"I have a dog here in Iraq that I am trying to get home to the US. . . I don't want [him] to get shot like the rest of the dogs around here . . . I was hoping maybe you could find a way to get him home before he becomes too big or disappears."

Or: ". . . she was crying and stuck in the barbed wire . . . I didn't see her mother anywhere and I couldn't leave her there to die."

Or: "My Company and I found a furry friend that has been with us through both the best of times and the very worst of times here in Iraq . . ."

Or: "If you would help me I would be forever in your debt."

What really got to Bonnie, though, was that for every service member Military Mascots helped, dozens more had to leave their pets behind. The service members had witnessed a lot of stuff. Bad stuff. Then they found these animals and couldn't bear to leave them behind. They became almost desperate to get them out.

One soldier in Baghdad contacted Bonnie and said he'd found three puppies who were orphaned after their mother was shot. Despite his best efforts during the following six months, all of the puppies died except one, who ended up being promoted by his troops to the rank of PFC after he survived being run over, electrocuted, and witness to 189 mortar rounds.

"We cannot leave him behind," the soldier wrote Bonnie.

But when the puppy's soldier redeployed, he could not find a safe ride for him from Baghdad to any border where Military Mascots could pick him up. The puppy remained behind in Baghdad at the base and hadn't been heard from since.

Then there was the pup found by a soldier in a garbage dump. The puppy slept with him, ate with him, patrolled with him wherever he went. The soldier's family sent food and toys for the puppy, and his nephew's school prayed daily for the puppy's safe return.

The soldier had big plans for the little guy when they got home. First he would take him to his nephew's school for a thank-you visit, then he would turn him loose in a big fenced yard, then he would let the pup have his choice of beds to sleep on in his new home.

But GO 1-A came down harder than hail that month and the soldier could no longer keep the puppy from being killed before he left for the United States. With no other options, the soldier took the puppy back to where he'd found him and left him there with promises from his comrades to feed him when they could.

Bonnie looked at the letter from Lieutenant Colonel Kopelman, though, and figured there was hope for this one. If he could get his puppy to Kuwait, she had a volunteer who could pick him up and put him on a plane to the States.

Still, she made it clear to the lieutenant colonel that Military Mascots did not support the movement of animals into the United States unless they were guaranteed a home with the service member's family.

"We realize that having your companion with you all these months has provided you with a 'touch of home' that you may have longed for," she wrote. "The sad fact is that the US is already filled with thousands of homeless animals and not enough good homes for them, therefore we want to know that your effort to bring your companion into the States has been an entirely thought out one and a lifetime commitment to your friend."

She also made it clear that getting the mascots home was a costly, time-consuming venture. A commercial flight and export fees into the States, for example, cost as much as fifteen hundred dollars from Iraq and twenty-five hundred from Afghanistan. The animal also needed an import/export permit, a health certificate, rabies and distemper vaccinations, and a shipping kennel.

She told Kopelman to give her volunteer a few days' notice of the puppy's arrival and work out a location for the pickup. She closed her e-mail message with the following quote from Ralph Waldo Emerson: "The purpose of life is not to be happy. It is to be useful, to be honorable, to be compassionate, to have it make some difference that you have lived and lived well."

She hoped this one worked out.

CHAPTER TWENTY-TWO

February 2005
Baghdad

ONCE A POSSIBLE exit route through Kuwait with Military Mascots is found, Sam makes it his mission to get Lava vaccinations and paperwork.

But in Baghdad, everything goes up for grabs. When the election results are finally announced in mid-February, Anne reports that Shiites and Kurds turned out the big winners, which means the Sunnis, who will be underrepresented in the new government, are more pissed off than hornets doused with water. Violence flares, and getting "proper documentation" for anything, let alone a puppy, beds down next to impossibility.

This is in part because in our rush to hand out private contracts for Iraq's reconstruction, oversight was shoveled away with just about everything else including sanity. The United States secretly awarded reconstruction projects, and US contractors earned excessive profits in part by subcontracting work to cheaper Iraqi companies, inflating charges, jimmying invoices, and welcoming kickbacks with bear hugs. They created shell companies in the Cayman Islands that falsely billed the US government. They paid ghost employees. They overpriced furniture contracts with kick-backs built right in and billed the government for products that were never delivered.

Embezzlement, payoffs, robberies. Later, a former senior adviser to the US-led Coalition Provisional Authority would say that Iraq was a "free fraud zone" as a result of the US government's refusal to prosecute contractors and companies accused of corruption. With no Iraqi law and no US law, the official said Baghdad was like the "Wild West." He told Congress that once he delivered two million dollars to a US contractor with bricks of cash in a bag.

On the Iraqis' side, public servants supplied salesmen and consumers with stolen medicine and medical equipment. Iraqi ministry officials pocketed millions in reconstruction money. Housing officials took bribes to allocate homes.

So, like I said, getting proper documentation for Lava is going to be tough.

First Sam finds someone who has the vaccine but won't sign the certificate of health because he doesn't want his name associated with helping Americans.

Then Sam finds someone who's willing to sign a certificate of health but doesn't have any vaccine.

Finally Sam locates a veterinarian who has the vaccine *and* is willing to sign the certificate, but he lives eight hours away from Baghdad and can't get there safely without a military escort, which even Sam, who can find puppy biscuits in Baghdad, cannot provide.

○

Anne is scheduled to leave for Cairo on February 26. She tells me she's trying to find a driver to take Lava to Kuwait.

I'm worried, though, because we just got word that Iraq's borders will be closed until February 23 for Ashura, a Shiite religious

Lava and me, shortly after he was found in an abandoned house in Fallujah, Iraq, November 2004. The puppy was rescued from certain death and was cared for by the Lava Dogs of 1st Battalion, 3rd Marine Regiment, from Kanehoe Bay, Hawaii.

Sergeant (then Corporal) Matt Hammond holds Lava In their barracks on Camp Fallujah. Sgt. Hammond was recovering from wounds he received during operations in Fallujah when he was hit by shrapnel from an insurgent's grenade. He nearly died from loss of blood, but recovered enough to stay at Camp Fallujah during his recovery, where he and Lava kept one another company. Despite his wounds, Hammond was determined to protect Lava from anyone who might want to remove the puppy from the camp, and Lava paid him back with a puppy's unconditional love. Today, both Hammond and Lava are doing well in southern California.

Lava, the destroyer, eyes a pair of sweatpants belonging to one of the Marines who cared for him at Camp Fallujah, the Marine base just outside the city of Fallujah. He no doubt thought they'd make a great chew toy.

A staple of Lava's early diet was beef jerky, which the Marines cut or tore into tiny pieces for the scruffy pup.

Waiting for a helicopter with my good friend Lieutenant Colonel "Buck" Liberto in September 2004. Only because Buck extended his tour of duty in Iraq was I able to have the opportunity to serve in Fallujah, where I met my new best friend, Lava.

A young Iraqi refugee seeks shelter and food at the Al Haidra mosque in Fallujah. The mosque quickly became a haven for displaced Iraqi families and infirm people. It also served as the center of the jobs program that Marines and their Iraqi counterparts organized to assist the people of Fallujah in getting back to self-sustenance.

MSG Dan Doyle and me, following a firefight in Fallujah.

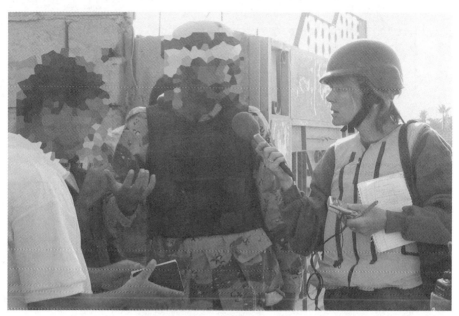

NPR correspondent Anne Garrels interviews an Iraqi soldier/interpreter outside a mosque in Fallujah, Iraq, November 2004. Annie was instrumental in caring for Lava and securing his evacuation from Iraq. We will be forever in her debt. *Note:* Faces of Iraqis are obscured throughout for their protection.

Major Chris Curtin and I stand on the berm at the Iraqi border where it intersects the borders of Iraq, Jordan, and Syria.

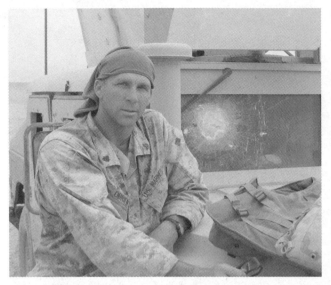

Marine sergeant Tim O'Brien following a particularly ferocious firefight. His actions that day while manning a MK-19 grenade launcher atop the team's High Mobility Multi-purpose Wheeled Vehicle (HMMWV, or Humvee) no doubt saved countless lives. Sergeant O'Brien braved an onslaught of enemy fire from an exposed position to ensure that his comrades could get into position to repel the insurgents' attack.

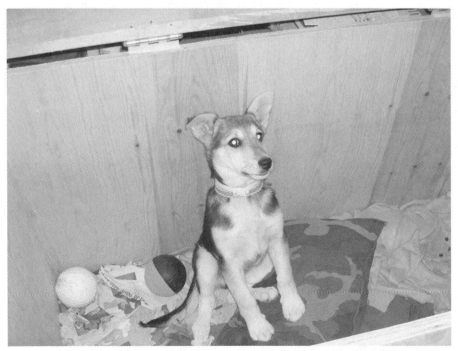

Lava's new digs at Camp Fallujah. Mat Hammond enlisted the expertise and skills of the local Seabees, who built this crate for Lava. The Marines caring for Lava filled it with blankets and toys, and when he grew too large to live inside, prepared it as a doghouse in the area behind their quarters.

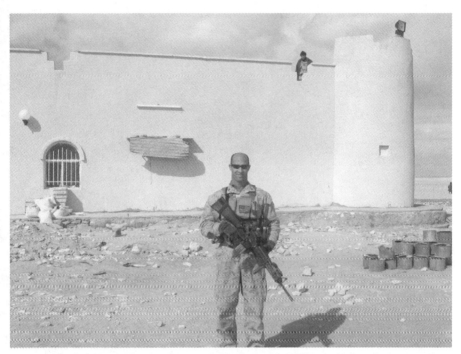

Standing in front of a border fort that was occupied by the Iraqi Special Border Police, also known as the Desert Wolves. There are many such forts now along Iraq's borders with Syria, Jordan, and Saudi Arabia. The Iraqi forces man these forts to ensure that no insurgents are entering Iraq at unmanned points.

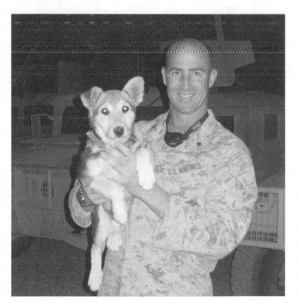

Saying goodbye to my new best friend in January 2005, just minutes before I boarded a helicopter that would take me to the Iraqi border with Syria. I didn't know—nor did I believe—I'd ever see the little guy again.

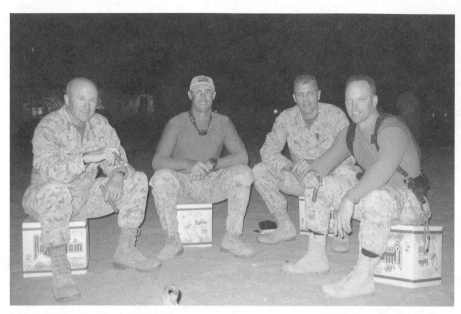

Waiting for our "freedom bird" in Kuwait, March 2005. All forces flowing into and out of the area are required to stop in Kuwait when they arrive and when they depart.

Lava with John Van Zante, the Director of Public Relations at the Helen Woodward Animal Center in Rancho Santa Fe, California. John's tireless efforts and transcontinental coordination ensured that Lava would one day enjoy a life in America. PHOTO BY KRIS PARLETT.

Lava with Kris Parlett, the community relations director for Iams pet foods. Kris worked very closely with John Van Zante to secure Lava's release and introduced John to Vohne Liche Kennels, who were so critical to Lava's journey to the United States. Iams graciously paid for Lava's travel home. PHOTO BY JOHN VAN ZANTE.

Lava with Ken Licklider, the owner of Vohne Liche Kennels, and his family, immediately following Lava's arrival at O'Hare Airport in Chicago. VLK raises and trains dogs for detection and protection work with the military and various law enforcement agencies. Lava flew to America with a shipment of the kennel's dogs who were coming home for a much-deserved period of rest and relaxation. PHOTO BY KRIS PARLETT.

Lava and his new "stepsister," Koda, at the park in La Jolla, California, where they first met in September 2005.

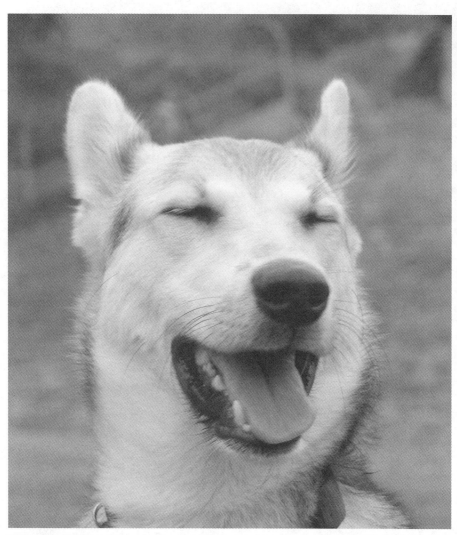

You'd laugh, too, if you'd gone from near certain death to living the good life in La Jolla, California. Here Lava is pictured lapping up the sun's rays. PHOTO BY CATHY JONES.

festival when tens of thousands of Muslims go on pilgrimage to the holy cities of Najaf and Karbala.

○

Sam does it somehow, though. He turns up one day at the NPR compound waving Lava's documentation papers—which, while wildly suspect, are proper documentation nonetheless, and that's good enough for Anne and me.

I don't ask for details, and all Sam says about it is: "I wish it was as easy to get a person out of Iraq."

○

Anne e-mails Bonnie and me:

> *I am working on getting Lava by car to Kuwait. I am just trying to confirm exactly what documents I need to get across the border, though I'm assured a $50 bill would probably be enough. I will know in a couple of days and then will let you know when to expect him in Amman and what documents he will be traveling with . . . I will miss him but am anxious to make sure he has a good home before I am no longer here to take care of him.*

Then I get an e-mail from John Van Zante confirming that Iams will make arrangements to get Lava on a flight out of Kuwait once they know the details of the handoff. John tells me he will meet Lava at the airport himself.

So I'm sitting at the Syrian border thinking everything's going to work out just fine, right? I'm already planning my own trip home in one month and thinking about how the first thing I'm going to do when I get there is take Lava to the beach.

I e-mail John: "It looks like Annie will get Lava to Kuwait where he will be picked up by one of the people from Military Mascots and put on a plane, most likely LAX. I'll provide the itinerary when I know it. I should be home about a month after Lava if all goes well for us both."

I e-mail Bonnie: ". . . John will be the one picking up Lava . . ."

I e-mail Annie: "Everything is good to go . . ."

Then Anne e-mails me back with news I should have learned to expect by now.

"I am somewhat at my wit's end. This is a great deal more complicated than we all anticipated . . ."

Those are the kind of words that make you think luck is tightening barbed wire around your balls just for shits and grins.

Apparently, Military Mascots usually receives animals from Iraq via a military convoy. When Bonnie realizes Lava will be coming with a private citizen in a private car, she writes Annie that the driver won't be allowed to cross into Kuwait and Bonnie's volunteer in Kuwait won't be allowed to cross over into Iraq.

In other words, the plan sucks. It won't work. Without a military escort, Lava can't get across the border.

I sit there and stare at the computer.

CHAPTER TWENTY-THREE

February 2005
The Syrian Border

MAYBE THIS SOUNDS selfish, but I don't want to die. Wanting to live is just one of those quirks of human nature that gets in the way of being a really good Marine, and besides, what else is there to do?

I want to live for various reasons: because I don't like pain, and getting killed will probably hurt; because I'm a little concerned that Hell might actually exist; and, at the risk of sounding like a complete martyr, because I'm worried about what will happen to Lava.

Once, back at Camp Fallujah, I went to see Lava at the Lava Dogs' building and passed by the Mortuary Affairs tent, the one with the DO NOT ENTER sign in front, and saw bodies being brought in and thought whoever was in that bag—they call them "human remains pouches"—was wearing the same uniform I had on. I wondered what they went through before they died and felt sorry they had to go through it but was glad it wasn't me.

It's not like they don't treat you well once you're dead or anything; you actually get quite a bit of respect and attention. They bring you in, put you on a concrete floor, and one guy checks for unexploded weapons and shrapnel with a metal detector, another guy sorts through your personal belongings, and two more look for identifying details—scars, tattoos, dog tags—and record things like how badly you were burned or how wide the puncture wound was or how well your bulletproof vest worked.

Meanwhile two other guys are writing it all down into a logbook. Then you're given an "evacuation number," put back into a human remains pouch, and sent to a camouflage refrigerator. It all takes about fifteen minutes.

The guys in the tent also process the remains of Iraqis—whether they're our soldiers, civilians, or insurgents—the theory being that once they're dead, they're no longer an enemy.

So they get the same treatment with identification and personal belongings, only they also get their picture taken, because they'll be sent back to the outskirts of Fallujah where they will be placed in one of the hundred-foot-long trenches we've dug with backhoes and bulldozers facing east toward Mecca. Each of these trenches is recorded with global positioning system coordinates, so family members know where to look for them later, after we're gone I guess.

The guys in the tent respect your body whether you're a Marine or an Iraqi. They never reach over it or lay anything on top of it, and they close your eyes and mouth if they're still open, which makes me wonder, as I'm passing by the tent, what it's like to die with your eyes open and, like, whether some computer engineer can come up with a way to read what's on a dead person's open eyeballs and play it back for the rest of us someday, because we all want to know what it's like to die.

When I get to the Lava Dogs' building, Lava rushes up to me and starts peeing, so I pick him up and take him outside and remind him that good Marines only pee outside. Only by that time he's finished, dribbled all over my uniform on the way out the door, so he's hopping up and down ready to play.

He's like that. No matter what Lava does, he does it full throttle. When he eats, he inhales. When he's lonely, he wails. When he's tired, he drops and snores within seconds. When he wants to play, he hops up and down in front of you, bites at your bootlaces, doesn't quit, doesn't apologize, just throws everything he's got into getting your attention.

Only I don't feel like playing. I sit on the ground and pull him onto my lap, where he rolls upside down with his paws up in the air. It's warm, right? And there's a lot of sun and as I'm sitting there rubbing his little belly and his legs stretch up, I start thinking about what will happen to him if I die.

It's kind of this noble thought wrapped up in selfishness, because I can't imagine *not* being alive somewhere once I'm dead. Hopefully I'll be up in Heaven looking down, only if I'm up there, and he's down here getting shot or drowned or wandering around on his own trying to find food, it won't matter that I've made it to Heaven and should be feeling eternally jubilant and healthy, because I'll be feeling guilty as hell instead.

Iraq has these unbelievable clouds. When you sit in the middle of the desert and look up, you're in a painting. It's too cool to be real, so I turn Lava upright and point toward the sky. He follows my fingers toward the tubes of white and blue.

"Pick out your cloud, buddy. Pick out your cloud."

CHAPTER TWENTY-FOUR

February 2005
The Syrian Border

I FEEL PRETTY bad for John Van Zante right about now, because we're starting to panic and look to him for any answers.

First I e-mail him and tell him about how the Iraqi drivers are not allowed by law to cross into Kuwait to drop Lava off, and the people in Kuwait can't come into Iraq.

"It's not looking good for Lava right now," I write.

Then Annie e-mails him and tells him she's leaving for Cairo in a few days and asks if there's anything else he can do from his end.

"Unfortunately, time is running out. I am extremely attached to this animal . . . I am afraid of what will happen to him here once I leave."

Then I e-mail John again: "I'm running out of ideas . . ."

But the guy is unstoppable. Even when I start feeling like maybe this is the end, like we've run out of chances (and this whole thing has been based on chance: *Chances are that . . . There's a slight chance that . . . If by chance we can . . .*), John belts out pep talks—"Let's all remember to take deep breaths. It's going to happen"—and revs up his marketing strategy. He says he's named Lava's mission "Operation Get It Done" and is going to call the entire California congressional delegation again and write letters to Governor Schwarzenegger and President Bush and contact a kennel owner in Indiana who transports bomb dogs in and out of Baghdad.

I just got off the phone with Kris Parlett at Iams in Dayton. Kris says they are working with a guy who is shipping pet food and other supplies to Iraq all the time. He's wondering if it would be possible to get Lava onto one of the transport planes. He's also checking on other Iams personnel in that part of the world. They have a major corporate facility in Switzerland as well as Iams distributors in Kuwait, Iraq, and Jordan.

Then he adds that if we can get Lava to Jordan somehow, Delta Air Lines might also be able to get him on a flight out from there, and John can pick him up wherever he lands in the United States.

This feels like good progress! We'll keep our paws crossed that we could still get him out on a commercial flight or transport plane . . . Mike Arms told me to keep a bag packed and be prepared to fly!

And I start thinking about this, about the chances of getting Lava to Jordan and on a flight out of Amman. It would be tough, though, a thousand kilometers from Baghdad across the "Wild West" of Iraq, only to face more chance at the border itself.

Here at Al Walid, the port of entry between Iraq and Syria, there is a congested one-lane checkpoint of sorts where we occasionally focus on ". . . so-and-so who will try to cross in an orange and white taxi . . ." or "such-and-such a truck smuggling oil out of Iraq" but mainly on vehicles with suspiciously low back ends and on any military-aged males trying to get through. For the most part, not much is happening at Al Walid.

The border crossing at Jordan is something different. The highway between Baghdad and Amman is traveled by refugees, gasoline smugglers, explosives-strapped camels, and suicide bombers stalking valuable, vulnerable military convoys. So security is tight. While the border itself is a thin line on the map, the column of vehicles crossing over stretches for miles in either direction. People sleep in their cars for days at the border. You can't even bribe your way into Jordan anymore.

There's another problem: Because of a rabies outbreak in Iraq, new laws restrict the flow of animals into Jordan. Lava has the paperwork, but I've heard that no animals are being let in at all.

There's a chance, though. If I can meet them at the border, I can probably help get him across. So I e-mail Annie and ask her for one more favor.

CHAPTER TWENTY-FIVE

February 2005
The Jordanian Border

ONE THING THAT scares even the most seasoned Iraqi driver is passing through checkpoints before crossing over borders. The insurgency hates the Iraqi soldiers and Iraqi civilians who work for us, and because both are so concentrated at the checkpoints, suicide bombers detonate there regularly.

The other thing they're afraid of is the US military and the Iraqi police who guard the checkpoints. It's a tense situation when you pull up and they start checking your vehicle, because if you make one wrong move, like sneeze, they're liable to think you're triggering an explosive and take all kinds of proactive action.

But Annie makes arrangements to get Lava on a flight out of Jordan to the States and then finds a driver who, even when she explains the job and the likely problems with the border crossing, shrugs and says in broken English, "Sure, no big deal. Everything can be solved with money"—implying that if he is paid well enough and has enough extra for bribes, he can help anyone sneak a little puppy through.

So you don't have to give your imagination much of a workout about what's going through the driver's head when Annie walks out of the compound with this puppy, bends down to say good-bye, and starts crying into his fur: *Easiest money I'll make for a* long *time to come.*

Only Lava isn't so little anymore, twenty-two pounds to be exact, and when Annie walks him over to the SUV and he sees the driver open the back and unlatch a crate, Lava stops and raises his hackles. Annie thinks he's going to start his *roo-roo-rooing*, right? Only he lowers his head, keeping his eyes on the driver, and gives out this low, deep-down growl instead.

The driver eyes him and smirks. He opens the crate. Lava shows his teeth.

Annie can't figure out what's going on. "Lava?" She's never seen him like this.

The driver smirks again.

Lava lunges.

Annie tries to grab him, but he flies through her hands and goes for the guy, who steps back, widens his eyes, and then takes off running around the SUV with Lava in pursuit. They circle twice before Annie is able to intervene.

By the time she grabs Lava and shoves him into the crate, the driver's sweating, lobbing insults in Arabic, and trying to equate "easy money" and "vicious animal."

Lava's in the crate, foaming at the mouth.

Annie, who's apologizing and explaining that the puppy will have to be let out several times during the trip, looks through her pockets for more money.

○

I manage to work my way from the Syrian border to the Jordanian border on the day Lava is supposed to pass through. Annie describes the vehicle to me in an e-mail, so I figure I'll be there when they arrive and help whisk them through.

Only when I get there, I realize that there are two checkpoints they'll have to cross: one between Iraq and no-man's-land, which is a several-mile strip of desert that belongs to neither country, and then another checkpoint from no-man's-land into Jordan. While I think I can probably get them through the first, I have no control over what happens at the second.

On top of that, the borders have been closed for the previous four days because of the holiday, so the line of vehicles waiting to cross stretches back into the Iraqi desert for several miles. I know the vehicle I'm looking for is a black-and-white Chevy Suburban, but as I scan the line, there are black-and-white Suburbans as far as I can see.

The Chevy Suburban is a popular vehicle here. It's easily armored, so they sell like crazy these days. You can order them off the Internet, where the ads say things like "Optional Run-Flat tires increase survivability in case of an ambush" and "Floor of passenger compartment is armored to shield against fragmentation from 2 DM-51 German ordnance hand grenades or equivalent" and "Armor Level B6 with DM-51 hand grenade protected floors standard." They even show before-and-after photos of their shot-up products with slogans like "No casualties!" and "Let us bite the bullet—not you!"

So I start walking the line of Suburbans, and I look inside every one of them, and when I do, the people inside look back at me and none of them, not one, says a word. No one complains. No one glares. They're as afraid of me as they are of getting blown up, and you know they're seething inside and thinking *Who do these people think they are coming into our country and searching our cars and telling us where we can and cannot go?* Only they can't say it out loud, can't even look like the words are going through their heads, and that makes me feel like an asshole with a great big star-spangled A on my chest, which, unlike theirs, is fully armored.

I walk up and down the line three times and start sweating about it, because I don't see them. Maybe the driver didn't make it or maybe he dropped Lava off in the desert and ran with the money or maybe he's got Lava stashed in a trunk and because he doesn't know who I am, he isn't letting on, and while I'm pushing my head through windows saying, yelling after a while, "Dog? Do you have a *dog*?" the little guy is suffocating because the drivers are afraid of me, and I'm making them more afraid of me as I storm up and down yelling *Dog?* into their faces, making them targets and losing my cool.

Then I see a cluster of Suburbans I hadn't seen before, and even before I reach them I see a crate in the back of one of them and start running. I see the driver twitch, wipe the back of his neck, and look the other way, because like I said he doesn't have a clue who I am. All he knows is that this US Marine is running toward him yelling something and the American lady's dog in the backseat is going crazy and every person in line is now looking his way.

Lava tries ripping through the crate when he sees me, and the first thing I notice is that he's crapped all over the place. I yank the back of the Suburban open and let him out while I yell up at the driver for not taking proper care of *my dog*. But the guy doesn't understand what's going on. He thinks he's in trouble, and the more I yell at him, the more he starts to sweat, and the more he starts to sweat, the more I yell, until I think he's about to cry.

My nerves are fried, so I try to calm down, because I can see he's about to flee for his life.

"Just back the vehicle up, and pull around," I tell him, but he just keeps sweating and looking in his rearview mirror and mumbling stuff in Arabic to himself or God as Lava pees all over the Suburban's optional run-flat tires.

I tell him again and add sign language: "Back the vehicle *up* and pull a-*round*."

I want him to back up and then pull around to get to the front of the line, right? But he's panicking and not following my English very well and starts to pull forward instead. That's when I lose it, because if he draws attention to himself, he's likely to get himself, Lava, and me killed.

See, I've been drilled my entire adult life to switch from fifth to automatic when fear tries to grab you and the tires start spinning. If it screams, you scream back louder. If it fires, you fire back and don't miss. You can't let fear kidnap you, can't let that black bag anywhere near your head or it gets cut off, and if you don't fight back, the black bag slips down over your eyes, and you start to panic and you start to pray, because you know you've just seen the last thing besides the inside of a black bag that you are ever going to see.

We make it to the front of the line eventually. I manage to calm down and point the driver in the right direction, and I walk up the line with Lava.

I can't believe how much he's grown, he's like a real dog now, and I start to feel pretty cool as we're walking and the Iraqis in line back away from us because they think he's a bomb dog.

Lava thinks it's cool, too. You can just see it sinking in. At first he's all puppy-like with me, jumping up and down trying to tell me how awful the ride was, but then, as the sea of people parts to let us through, he gets all serious and starts moving his head back and forth with an authoritative air calculated to let everyone know he's got his eye on them.

At one point, I can't help it, I think of Annie's e-mail and tell Lava to *sit*. He doesn't even look up at me, just stops, sits, and continues his bomb-dog gaze at the crowd. I try to look all stern, like I suspect something's up, but I have no idea what a military dog handler says to his dog at a time like this, so I say "Lava, *search*" and try to make it sound official, because everyone's staring at us, and I'm feeling pretty cool.

When we get to the front of the line, the driver is trying to explain to a small battalion of guards who've surrounded his vehicle and are pointing weapons at him that the crazy Marine with the dog—"That one there," and he points to us with wide eyes—has *told* him to pull in front of everyone else.

I'm still pretty pissed at him and consider for more than a fraction of a second shrugging and saying I've never seen him before. I'm also worried that he's about to return every cent of the easiest money he's ever made and go home, so I let him see it cross my mind. He gets the message.

So do the guards when I wave the vaccination certificates around in their faces and tell them this vehicle *is* crossing.

I walk to the driver's side of the Suburban and give the guy a nod. It's not his fault that this happened to him—this situation, this country, this whole war that's so screwed up. He's not a soldier. He's not a suicide bomber. He probably worked at a dry cleaner before this all started.

"Thanks, man."

I look down the miles of humanity waiting to escape into no-man's-land, and at the Iraqi soldiers who, awkward with guns and swimming in US-issued cammies, are trying their best to act brave. None of them is at fault. They're afraid. We all are. It's just that some of us are too afraid to show how afraid we really are.

"And, uh, sorry."

I clean out the crate and hate like hell putting Lava back in. I can see confusion cross his face—*But I thought . . .*—and I feel like a traitor.

"It's okay, Lava, everything's going to be okay."

But I thought . . .

"You be a good boy."

But . . .

"Be nice to the driver. He's okay. I'll see you soon. I promise."

WAIT...

I close the back of the Suburban, pound on the back to let the driver know to take off, and then I turn away.

○

By the next morning I'm back at the Syrian border, where I open a new e-mail from Annie.

The driver, she says, made it through no-man's-land in one piece, but when he reached the Jordanian side of the checkpoint, he was turned away.

"Lava," she writes, "is back in Baghdad with me."

CHAPTER TWENTY-SIX

February 2005
The Syrian Border

THERE ARE DOZENS of stray dogs where I'm stationed at the border. I have no idea where they came from, either. We're in the middle of the desert.

They're all pretty skittish, but I feed a couple of them MREs and try to make friends. None of them lets me get close, so I put the food several dozen yards away from the building and watch them eat as the sun goes down.

It's funny, they all look the same from a distance except for this one, this black male with gold eyes who I figure is the leader of the group, because the others are watching him all the time. Like when I put the food out, they all pace and whine at the horizon, but the black male, he just sits and stares. When he estimates that I'm far enough from the food, he stands up and walks over while the others go still and just watch him.

His reward for being the first to go in is that he gets to eat before the others. While I know they're all starving, they let him eat first. If one of them can't stand the wait and gets too close to the food while he's still eating, all he has to do is give them a look, and they back off. No bullying. No gnashing of teeth. Just this calm stare.

And without exception, every single time, the black male eats a little bit and then walks off as if bored with the whole business even though you know he hasn't had his fill. Then and only then do the others attack the food until every scrap is gone. It's like they know they can trust him to face the danger first, and then they know they can trust him to let them all eat. The pack, as a result, survives.

And as I'm watching this, I start thinking about the Iraqi soldiers who cringe and avoid eye contact when I yell at them for breaking the rules. They drive me crazy, because no matter how much I scream about how breaking the rules hurts the strength of the unit, they'll still steal candy when they think they can get away with it.

Then it dawns on me: I don't want submission; I want loyalty. But to gain their loyalty, I have to gain their trust, and I don't gain their trust, because I'm always flying off the handle and losing control.

This black male dog, though, he's got it figured out. All he has to do is stare, and the others do what he wants. I start calling him Jacki the Iraqi and decide I want to pet him someday.

I just can't figure out where they came from. Same thing with all the stray dogs back at Camp Fallujah. Where were they born, and how did they end up in the middle of nowhere?

The puppies that Matt Hammond and Lava found in the sewer were probably born to a stray who got caught in one of the animal control traps, but where did the mother come from and where did her mother come from?

Her puppies lucked out big time when the Marines found them, I guess; they got fed for a little while longer anyway. Then one day the sewer was filled up with dirt, like someone was told to kill the puppies but couldn't make himself do it, so he just covered the whole situation over and walked away.

When Matt found the sewer like that, he could hear the puppies still whimpering through the dirt, so he and six other Marines started digging to get them out. They scratched and clawed with their hands, pickaxes, and shovels as dirt and sand flew from one Marine into the face of another until it started to get dark and some of the guys had to hold flashlights so the others could see what they were doing. Then someone yelled "Found one," and the flashlight beams all fixed on something still alive, and it was the closest they'd ever come to giving birth.

They brought the puppies back to the building and took care of them there for a while, but one day when the whole team had to leave for a couple of hours, someone under orders snuck into the building and took them all away. Later they were told it was for "health reasons."

At least they didn't die buried alive.

I don't know what's going to happen to these strays here at the border once I leave for the States in a couple of weeks. I suppose they'll survive somehow. But jeez, what a way to live, always starving, always afraid, always heading toward death no matter how hard they try, like slowly suffocating, like being buried alive.

And what about the Iraqis, what's going to happen when we leave? It's still too hard to tell if they'll dig themselves out of the dirt we've buried them in, but if they don't, it won't be because the Iraqi soldiers in US cammies weren't yelled at enough; it will be because they never trusted us in the first place.

As for Lava, he's been well fed and well trained, but he can't make it on his own. He's tough but not that tough.

It's pretty late at night when I write Annie an e-mail:

"Try not to let this frustrate you too much. You've done all that you can and then some to help Lava and me. I appreciate it more than you know."

Then I tell her that maybe the best solution is to have the little guy euthanized. It's better than being buried alive.

CHAPTER TWENTY-SEVEN

February 2005
The Syrian Border

MISERY LOVES COMPANY, but during the whole time we tried to get Lava out of Iraq, I don't think it ever paid a visit to John Van Zante. While the failure at the Jordanian border explodes in my face and causes all kinds of internal injuries from which I doubt I will ever recover, it blows right past John in a thin layer of dust.

Despite the fact that we cannot find an exit route for Lava, that Anne is leaving Baghdad in twenty-four hours, that I'm stuck here at the Syrian border until I leave for the States in several weeks, and that Lava has no place to go, John sends me an e-mail full of enthusiasm and exclamation points.

"We're waiting to hear back today from the folks at Vohne Liche Kennels . . ."

The who? The what?

"I don't want to give false hope, but on Thursday they just seemed to think it was no big deal . . ."

I vaguely remember John mentioning a kennel in Indiana or something, but in the chaos surrounding the Kuwait and Jordan escape plans I didn't pay much attention. At the time it was just another of John's shots in the dark aimed in the same general direction as his letters to Governor Schwarzenegger and President Bush.

"In our last contact with them on Thursday, they said that Kenneth Licklider, the owner, was very excited about helping out."

I'm scrounging my gray matter for whatever it was John told me earlier about this kennel, because I want the pieces to fit, but all I can remember is reading something about how Iams worked with this kennel or knew someone at this kennel and contacted them for information about smuggling a dog out of Iraq, only I can't remember exactly and wonder what a kennel owner in Indiana could do to help out, and more importantly, *why*?

O

Turns out, Ken Licklider, the guy who owns Vohne Liche Kennels, is a former US Air Force police dog handler who trains police dogs for tracking, apprehension, search, and seizure work. He specializes in explosives passive response work, and many of his dogs are used by the US military to sniff out bombs in Iraq.

His kennel in Indiana trains four hundred dogs and 150 handlers from twenty different countries every year. Like, the guy's famous for what he can do with dogs. He provided security for President Reagan, three presidential candidates, the Olympic Games in Los Angeles, the pope's visit to LA, the Federal Reserve Bank, and the Internal Revenue Service.

I guess the US State Department figured that if a guy can provide security for the pope and the IRS, he's probably pretty good, so they hired him to provide protection for Afghanistan's President Karzai, and as testament to how good Ken is, the president continues to live.

So when Ken gets a call from Iams and hears about how these Marines found this puppy in Fallujah and how this lieutenant colonel snuck him back to the base camp and how the camp general's personal security detail and some navy Seabees hid him and how an American journalist now has him stashed in Baghdad and how we seem to fail at every turn to get him out—the political failure and the military-flight failure, the Kuwait failure, and the Jordanian failure—the guy doesn't even blink.

"Sure I can do it. I can get a dog out."

He and his crew and their dogs fly in and out of Iraq all the time.

○

"It just means putting Lava on a transport with their dogs and handlers and flying him back," John tells me.

Ken also tells John that it's probably *better* that Lava didn't make it through Jordan, because most of their guys fly in and out of Baghdad anyway. All we have to do, it seems, is get Lava from the Red Zone to the military base in the Green Zone, and they'll take it from there.

Sounds too simple.

CHAPTER TWENTY-EIGHT

February 2005
Baghdad

ANNE IS IN Baghdad getting ready to leave for Egypt and feeling as worried about Lava as I am and reporting one of her last stories about how out of the eighteen billion dollars set aside by the United States for Iraqi reconstruction, only three billion has been paid out so far.

". . . a group of twelve US soldiers prepares to venture past the concrete blast wall, sandbags, and guard posts that separate them from the Red Zone—the rest of Baghdad," she reports, adding that standing with them is a US civilian contractor whom the military convoy is assigned to protect.

The contractor, in a Kevlar helmet and flak jacket, has until October to hand out eleven million in US aid to help small businesses in Baghdad get back on their feet. But in the three months that he's been here, he's only gotten paperwork done for about five thousand dollars in grants, because every time he steps out of the Green Zone, someone tries to kill him.

Every day, the contractor climbs into an up-armored Humvee with a machine-gun turret on top and travels through the Red Zone trying to hand out money. If he finds a likely candidate, he figures he has about ten minutes to make his pitch before someone sees the candidate talking to a westerner and opens fire.

Before the convoy takes off, Anne records the commander's briefing to his twelve soldiers: "When we're out on the road, action on contact. We engage in small-arms fire when gunner can positively identify the source, then go ahead and engage . . ."

Anyway, I don't know what she said, I don't know what she threatened or promised during her last days in Baghdad, but she e-mails me at the last minute that her replacement, Anthony Kuhn, has agreed to watch Lava at the NPR compound for the next several weeks until he leaves in the middle of March.

Two weeks. We have two more weeks. I'm beginning to feel lucky. And fully bipolar.

○

I contact John and tell him the news and then write a note to Ken Licklider, the owner of Vohne Liche Kennels, to introduce myself and tell him Lava is ready to leave Iraq.

"Sir," he responds, "we have people rotating back at the end of the month that may be able to help you. I am contacting my on-site supervisor there in the Green Zone, a Mr. David Mack, and asking him to do what he can . . . Just make sure the dog has a health certificate."

That makes me cringe, because I don't know exactly how legitimate Lava's paperwork is, so when I first hear from David Mack, who's worked for Vohne Liche for three years in Afghanistan and Iraq and manages the kennel's dog teams in overseas missions, I forget to mention anything about it.

○

Meanwhile, Anne reports her last story from Baghdad, about how the US-funded, state-run television station is airing a series of confessions by insurgents who claim they were financed and trained by the Syrian government.

They say they were trained in explosives and beheadings. They say they were ordered to cause chaos in Iraq. They say they had to kill at least ten Iraqi soldiers each, and an additional ten dollars was thrown in for each one they beheaded as long as they caught it on film.

I don't know if she'd admit it, but Annie *needs* to get out of this place for a while. You can only struggle in quicksand for so long before you get sucked under. I'm happy for her. I'm glad she's getting out, but I'm still worried about Lava, because Annie's known him as long as I have, and I never worried she'd do anything but her best.

Thank you, Annie. I know how hard it was for you to leave the little guy behind, and thank you.

○

John Van Zante, David Mack, Anthony Kuhn, and I begin a round of e-mails to figure out how to get Lava from one set of hands to the other.

David: "We will try to move Lava out at the end of the month. We have several dog guys going back on or around the 30th, so we will try to arrange for those guys to escort Lava at that time."

Anthony: "I'm heading back to London on Friday the 18th. My colleague Lourdes 'Lulu' Garcia-Navarro will be here as of Thursday the 17th. Our producer, Ben Gilbert, is here, too. Lava's in fine shape and we'll do whatever is needed to get him to the Green Zone safe and sound."

John: ". . . will it be possible for someone from Vohne Liche to reach Jay or the NPR people on cell phone in the event that they can arrange to transport Lava into the Green Zone or the [military] base in the Green Zone? We realize that cell phone time is valuable, and we do not want to jeopardize anyone's safety or security, but we're thinking ahead. Don't want to be in a situation where Lava can get on a plane, but can't get on base."

Me: "John, I am 99.9% certain that the NPR folks won't be able to get Lava to the base in the Green Zone without a pass. The most likely scenario would be to have the NPR folks meet the Vohne Liche folks at the *entrance* to the Green Zone."

David: "I will contact you again when I will need to have Lava brought to me in the Green Zone . . . I will let you know more in a couple of days."

Ben Gilbert, the NPR producer at the compound, chimes in at one point: "There's been a ton of e-mail traffic on this, so I'm a bit unclear on who is who . . ."

John: "If I understand this all correctly, here's what's happening: NPR's Lourdes 'Lulu' Garcia-Navarro gets to Baghdad on the 17th; NPR's Anthony Kuhn leaves on the 18th and Lava stays in the Red Zone; Vohne Liche's David Mack would like to have Lava delivered to him in the Green Zone by the 29th; On or about the 30th, David will get Lava moved to Baghdad International Airport (BIAP) where he will link up with the Vohne Liche guys going home; Once he's on the plane he'll fly from BIAP to Chicago; When he lands in Chicago, Lava can be picked up by someone from the Vohne Liche staff or one of us."

Me: "Thanks, John."

John: "We've been close so many times. This one seems like it's as near as we've come to actually putting Lava on a plane and getting his furry little butt out of Iraq . . . I hope this is it!!!!"

But then the final kick comes.

David: "Can you confirm that Lava has all his health & shot papers in order? Recently we ran into a vaccination problem with one of our dogs & the military vet would not allow the dog to leave the country for an extra 30 days.

"I don't want to see that happen to Lava."

And it hits in the solar plexus, because everyone, including me, is leaving soon, and Lava doesn't have thirty days.

CHAPTER TWENTY-NINE

March 2005
Shannon, Ireland

IT'S FIVE THIRTY in the morning in a Shannon pub where a bunch of Marines around me punch each other in the arms, sing Irish folk songs, and make the bartender nervous as hell while I sit and gaze at the empty bottom of, like, my third or fourth pint of Guinness, which has to be the most bitter thing I've ever put in my body. I'm pretty sure it's just a mixture of refined gasoline and molasses, but it takes a full twelve minutes of pulling and settling, pulling and settling before the bartender even serves it to you, and by that time you're so thirsty and worried about your guys causing trouble, you all but get on your knees and give thanks when it arrives.

"And the band played Waltzing Matilda as the ship pulled away from the quay . . ." I'd really like to tell the guys to shut up, but I don't, because I'm fairly impressed that they even know the words.

So I order another pint and carve grit out from under my fingernails with my teeth while I wait. It's about the only thing I have with me from Iraq, the grit, only it's probably not even grit from Iraq but from Kuwait, which is where we stayed for three days in a tent before we flew here to Shannon.

"And the band played Waltzing Matilda as we stopped to bury our slain . . ."

We're on our way home, and we've just spent a year or more inhaling sand, and we fly into this country that's as moist and green as an ocean and everyone's all strung out from lack of sleep, wired about eating real food, wired about having sex again, and this unfortunate bartender is serving us our first alcohol as free men and listening to foreigners butcher Matilda. Jeez, we've got balls, don't we? I wonder what these guys would do if they were standing behind a bar listening to a bunch of drunk Iraqis sing "Leaving on a Jet Plane."

I don't know how long it's been since I flew from the Syrian border back to Camp Fallujah and then on to Kuwait and then here. Days? Weeks? I don't know. I don't care. I just want to get drunk and sleep for a while. I feel tired and itchy and dirty, like you do when you get back from patrolling the desert and the dust and the sand and the dirt fornicate with sweat under your collar and you'd do just about anything to get under a shower to wash it away. All you want is a shower. All I want right *now* is a shower.

By the time I got to Camp Fallujah from the Syrian border, Matt Hammond is already back in the States undergoing multiple surgeries for his wounds, thirty-one of the Lava Dogs are dead from the helicopter crash, hundreds of other Marines are on their way home in flag-wrapped boxes, and a whole new group of young Iraqi guys is being fitted with US cammies.

"For to hang tents and pegs a man needs two legs, no more Waltzing Matilda for me . . ."

If this had been a year ago, I would have arrived at Camp Fallujah feeling like I'd returned to a party at 4 AM to find the music down and everyone passed out. One year ago I would have felt the "best" of the fighting had turned from Fallujah to Baghdad and would have done just about anything to get transferred there. But I'm one year older now, and it all seems like the funeral just about to begin, and the only reason I want to go to Baghdad is to see Lava one more time. Other than that, I'd just as soon go home.

I don't plan on Lava making it back to California. I don't think about where he's going to sleep or which beaches allows dogs or what veterinarian I'm going to take him to. I just fill out my paperwork, make sure I ingest the proper number of calories, and take, like, one million showers.

See, the plan to fly him out with the Vohne Liche folks is too simple. It's too easy to make sense. Too many people love him, and no one, not even a Lava Dog, can be so lucky.

Luck—you hope for it, you pray for it, you break laws to find it, because unlike drilling and practicing and following all the rules, it allows you for one fraction of one fraction of a second to strut along the sidelines like the Ref and control the uncontrollable events in your life.

"And the band plays Waltzing Matilda, and the old men still answer the call. Year after year, their numbers get fewer, someday no one will march there at all."

But you only get so much luck, that's my theory these days, and the fact that I'm still alive, the fact that I'm just about to get my fifth pint of Guinness in a pub in Ireland at five forty-five in the morning while my comrades get louder and the bartender gets sterner and I get drunker, means I'm probably scraping the bottom of the barrel.

CHAPTER THIRTY

March 2005
Baghdad

AT 1113 COMPOUND in the Green Zone, David Mack looks over the list of Lava's paperwork Ben e-mailed him this morning. It can't be legitimate, can it?

He scans Lava's documentation from the perspective of the checkpoint patrols who will decide the puppy's fate by either letting him cross into the Green Zone or turning him away. It includes an International Health Veterinary Certificate for Live Animals from the Ministry of Agriculture of the Republic of Iraq—a translated document, signed and certified, with the original in Arabic attached—and an International Certificate of Vaccination and Health for Dogs.

"This is all I have," Ben wrote.

While it looks pretty good, David wonders how they managed to get it.

○

At the NPR compound in the Red Zone, Sam teaches Lava some of the finer points of soccer so that when he emigrates to the United States, he will represent Iraq well.

Lava still hasn't grown into the leather belt that overwhelms his neck, but Sam tells him it makes him different from the other dogs wandering around Baghdad and that he should wear it like a uniform and be proud.

"Lava is happy," Ben Gilbert writes.

○

If Ben Gilbert can get Lava through the first checkpoint between the Red Zone and the Green Zone on March 29, he'll meet David Mack on Saddam Hussein's parade grounds near the *Hands of Victory* Monument. From there David will get Lava on a private convoy to the airport and into the hands of a Triple Canopy dog handler, Brad Ridenour, who's scheduled to fly with some of Vohne Liche's dogs back to the States where they will get a long-deserved rest from sniffing out bombs.

While getting Lava across the checkpoint between the Red Zone and the Green Zone will prove the most technically difficult part of the rescue, the trip to the airport will be the most physically danger-ous by far. An entire Marine battalion patrols the four-lane, six-mile road leading from the Green Zone to Baghdad International Airport, but because the highway is one of the most vital supply routes in Iraq for the US military and private contractors and is traversed daily by convoys of Marines, businessmen, and journalists, it's considered "target-rich" by the insurgency.

In the past two months alone, dozens of people have been killed on the highway by roadside bombs, sniper bullets, suicide bombers, private security contractors, and the US military itself. It is called the Road of Death.

○

At the NPR compound, Anne's replacement, Anthony Kuhn, files one of his last stories before he leaves Baghdad. It's about the release of Giuliana Sgrena, the Italian journalist who was abducted by insurgents just before Anne left, and about how speeding on her way to the Baghdad International Airport with the two men who negotiated her release, their Toyota Corolla was targeted and hit.

Sgrena, who'd just spent one month in a dark room courtesy of the Islamic Jihad Organization, was hit in the shoulder by shrapnel. One of the mediators who sat next to her in the backseat, Nicola Calipari, was shot in the head and killed.

Only it wasn't the insurgency this time. It was a US tank posted on the road to protect a convoy transporting US ambassador John Negroponte to the airport.

"Late Friday, President Bush spoke by phone from *Air Force One* with Prime Minister Silvio Berlusconi," Kuhn reports, adding that the president expressed "regret" at the incident and pledged a full investigation.

"Italian politicians criticized the incident and Sgrena's newspaper, *Il Manifesto*, announced that instead of celebrating her return, an antiwar rally is now planned."

○

Ben Gilbert tells us that a journalist stationed in Baghdad by ABC heard about Lava and wants to do a story about his escape. The journalist, who has credentials to get through the Green Zone checkpoint, offered to escort Lava from the NPR compound to David Mack at Saddam Hussein's parade grounds if his station got an exclusive story from it.

Sam gets Lava ready and gives him another bath.

○

Meanwhile I'm stuck in the States at Camp Pendleton wondering when things changed so much that I now consider the United States of America a place in which to be stuck.

But stuck I am, and I'm reading all these e-mails and have no control over what's happening in them. It's like reading a book and all I can do to find out what happens in the end is turn the page.

CHAPTER THIRTY-ONE

March 2005
California

JOHN VAN ZANTE has to make the final flight arrangements for Chicago, but he needs to finish up the e-mail to members of the San Diego media about the dangers of Easter first.

"While this release is mainly about Easter plants that are toxic to pets . . . please see the note about why it's a TERRIBLE idea to buy bunnies and chicks for Easter."

Things finally seem to be going Lava's way. It is the closest they've come to getting him home.

"Remember that bunnies grow up to be rabbits that chew on everything, are subject to eye ailments, need their fur and nails clipped, and pee on everything!"

John has been on the phone for three days with Kris Parlett from Iams and Ken Licklider from Vohne Liche Kennels to map out the strategy: If Lava makes it from the Red Zone to the Green Zone and if he makes it from the Green Zone to the Baghdad airport and if he makes it from the Baghdad airport to the States, then the three of them will be waiting at O'Hare in Chicago when he arrives. The important part will be getting media at the airport in Chicago.

"Those cute, fuzzy baby chicks lose the fluff and it's replaced with feathers. Then they become chickens that cluck, crow, and poop.

"And when the bunnies and chicks become adults, their owners give them away, abandon them, or ignore them until they're too sick to survive."

What began four months ago as a mission to bring media attention to the center's Home 4 the Holidays event and homeless animals is now a personal mission to get Lava out of Iraq. But it's more than that.

When John heard that ABC was interested in doing a story about Lava's escape, he e-mailed everyone a list of names—Anne Garrels, Anthony Kuhn, Lourdes Garcia-Navarro, Ben Gilbert, Triple Canopy Security's dog handler Brad Ridenour—and asked who else should be publicly thanked.

Ben Gilbert wrote him back almost immediately.

Hi Everyone, I understand that a lot of people have gotten on board with this, but I would really appreciate it, that if there is a press conference of some sort, that someone mentions [Sam] who took care of Lava from the time he arrived in Baghdad. [Sam] got the shots for Lava. He got the doggie passport, the letter from the Ministry of Agriculture and went to the translator who certified the letter. He bought Lava biscuits, a toy, and most importantly . . . played with him, giving him much needed love and attention. [Sam] also tried to arrange previous trips for Lava's route through Jordan by car, kept 'doggedly' pursuing a way for Lava to find his way to the States . . .

So hats off to everyone for making this happen, but [Sam] has cared for Lava over the past month, and he is asking for nothing in return.

It would be a great honor to him to be mentioned on American TV as a contributor to this successful operation. I feel strongly about this.

I think it's more important for his name to be mentioned than NPR's.

John stares at his computer screen. One year ago, the dangers of Easter seemed important enough.

"We'll be happy to work with you on a story about this. Not all doom and gloom, but some positive reasons why bunnies and chicks are not good Easter gifts."

Now they seem absurd.

CHAPTER THIRTY-TWO

April 2005
California

I HEARD SOMEONE say once that passionate people live violent lives. At the time, I didn't really get it, but if what they meant was the way love waits in ambush, traps your well-trained sense of control, and then tortures you into a confession you'd just as soon not make, I now understand.

The first part of the confession is that I let Lava get to me. I unlocked my cool, let the little shit right in, and after that, all sorts of things seeped through, including fear. I mean, I guess it's fear that's doing this to me. Maybe it's just what the therapist calls post-traumatic stress, even though I've only been home for a week; or maybe it's just residue from the sleeping pills still floating through my bloodstream, or maybe some chemical imbalance brought on recently by any number of issues, but hell, what else besides fear could cause this much panic?

Anxiety, maybe. Anxiety assumes less culpability, implies less of an offense, offers more of an excuse. Or obsession, perhaps, but that implies a lifetime of prescription slips from the therapist, and besides, not everyone involved in the rescue—the Marines, the journalists, the Iraqis, the private security guys—could be crazy. Maybe they could. Nothing seems right-side up anymore and hasn't for some time now.

Maybe it's just compulsiveness. Along with nightmares, flashbacks, moodiness, alcoholism, and depression, they said something about a compulsive disorder that could send your brain cells scurrying into all sorts of witless directions, and between checking incoming e-mail, praying for the phone to ring, and counting the paces between one wall and the next, it seems entirely plausible.

But then, so did getting Lava out of Iraq in the first place, and how impeachable was that offense after Allah, Jehovah, Jesus, Lady Luck, and Santa Claus made it pretty clear it wasn't on their list of things to do this year?

I check the e-mail again. Nothing. It's the middle of the day there in Baghdad, the middle of the night here in California, and no time in particular to me everywhere else in between. Something must have gone wrong.

The second part of the confession is that once you let fear in, it's hard to get rid of, and the more you try, the deeper it digs its heels. Four months ago, I wasn't afraid of anything, at least that's how I remember it in comparison to now when I'm afraid of everything including the voice on my computer announcing new mail.

I think the pacing is what's getting to me. The back-and-forth unearths all kinds of radioactive crap I don't want hanging around. Like a lot of faces. Weird, dreamy faces. Faces of stray dogs I fed at the Syrian border. Faces of embedded journalists in Fallujah with terror dripping down them like sweat. Faces of Iraqis smashed into the street like ripe banana meat under your boot and the question of whether a face is really a face if there's no one home behind it.

Mostly, though, faces of people who risked their lives to try to save Lava. They bother me the most. I think we all let the mangy little flea-bitten refugee get to us—as if love were some sinister germ intent on infection—and now that we've all been bitten by the contagion, now that it comes down to the end, now that all other roads of escape are closed for good, I feel I owe it to them to make sure Lava gets out alive.

Maybe the little shit is dead already. Or maybe they didn't make it through and he's now lost on the streets of Baghdad wondering where everybody went. I pray that if Lava doesn't make it through, he'll find a body somewhere in Baghdad to keep him alive for just one more day.

Which brings me to the last part of my confession: I want Lava to stay alive. No matter how bad things get, it's still better to be alive. I want to know he's breathing and leaping after dust balls and chasing imaginary enemies in his sleep. I want him to be alive, because then there's still hope that he'll make it here to California and get to be an American dog who runs on the beach and chases the mailman instead of strangers with guns. I want him to be alive almost more than anything I can think of, which feels like a confession, because before Lava, I was a Marine who wasn't required to cross any lines with ALIVE on one side and DEAD on the other. I carried a rucksack full of coupons redeemable towards absolution. Now, after meeting Lava and letting fear in, I feel distantly related to a serial killer.

CHAPTER THIRTY-THREE

April 2005

So THIS IS fear. This is what it all comes down to: waiting for an -
e-mail.

Fear's got nothing to do with pain or eternal damnation or
existence that's been canceled. There are no improvised explosive
devices in this arena. No trip wires or vulnerable porta-shitters or
sandstorms that take your chopper down.

Your own death has nothing much to do with it in the end. Ask
anyone who's been there the beheaded, the burned, the blown to
bits—I bet they'd give you an earful. Death, buddy, is death. Slit,
boom, bang. One minute you're alive; the next minute you're dead,
and once that happens, once you finally experience what you've worried about all your life, that's it. There's nothing else to worry about.

It's just all the in-between stuff. All the waiting.

○

At the NPR compound, Ben Gilbert puts Lava in a vehicle with the
ABC cameraman. They hide Lava (in ways that can't be detailed),
because no animals are allowed to pass from the Red Zone into the
Green.

Security around the Green Zone is cinched tighter than usual after a United Nations report indicated "irregularities" with the election, demonstrations raged, and insurgents fired mortar rounds into the Green Zone's concrete barrier. If they get to the checkpoint, and the driver doesn't look right, the vehicle is the wrong color, if Lava so much as farts, it's all over.

The vehicle takes off. Sam waves good-bye.

Meanwhile, across the city, a roadside bomb kills three Iraqi policemen and wounds five, a car bomb kills seven people and wounds nine, and more mortar rounds are launched into the Green Zone.

○

And I've gotten to wondering, as I sit here and wait for the e-mail to arrive, if that's what the suicide bombers tell themselves — that their lack of control over death makes everything *but* death a waste of energy. I mean, to blow yourself up has got to hurt, right? Even if it's only for a fraction of a second, there is still that fraction of a second to look forward to when your skin tears away from your bones and your brain goes one way and your toes go another and every form of torture devised by man comes together in one single fraction of a second that you've been hardwired to avoid since sperm met egg. But they do it anyway. They disconnect their own internal wiring and pull the detonator anyway.

And, I mean, you gotta ask: *Why?*

I figure they just get tired of waiting.

○

The vehicle speeds through the streets of the Red Zone without stopping as a videotape is posted on the Internet showing three Iraqis being executed for working for the US military and as a memo is released to the press indicating that a top US commander in Iraq authorized illegal interrogation tactics that included using military guard dogs to "exploit Arab fear of dogs."

○

The rest of us, we just pace back and forth, check our e-mail, stare at the computer, and worry about what's being arranged for us in some other galaxy. We wait. We worry. We wait.

○

The vehicle inches forward through the checkpoint line. Exhaust and heat vapors marbleize the air. The driver stares forward. The cameraman counts rolls in the concertina wire outside his window.

Over on the other side of town, dozens of insurgents attack the Abu Ghraib prison with car bombs and rocket-propelled grenades just as the US National Guard announces back home that it is easing restrictions on recruitment and now accepts anyone with at least a ninth-grade education.

○

Wait.

○

David Mack stands at the drop-off point in the Green Zone under the *Hands of Victory* Monument, a triumphal arch of two fists holding two swords made from the melted guns of Iraqi soldiers killed in the Iran–Iraq War that soar 140 feet into the air and meet in the middle where the helmets of captured Iranian soldiers hang in a net. The fists that hold the swords are replicas of Saddam's own hands. One of the thumbs on one of the hands replicates Saddam's own fingerprint.

Even at a time like this, you've got to admit that it makes a point.

○

Wait.

○

A bomb dog circles the vehicle as a guard reaches through the window and checks the cameraman's pass. The pass is good; it's the bomb dog detecting Lava that poses the threat.

But he's in search of only one thing. When he doesn't find it, he's off to the next vehicle. The guard scans the pass and waves them through into the Green Zone where, at that moment, the Iraqi government huddles behind the concrete barrier and extends the country's emergency state by an additional thirty days.

○

Wait.

○

Brad Ridenour's plane lands at Baghdad International Airport. John Van Zante's plane lands at O'Hare in Chicago. In Indiana, Ken Licklider checks his watch one last time.

○

Wait some more.

○

Iraqi police patrolling the parade grounds watch a vehicle trailing dust approach the *Hands of Victory* Monument and stop. They watch one man get out of the vehicle and shake hands with another, watch the two men exchange some papers, watch a dog jump out of the car.

They approach the vehicle. They ask to see the papers. They ask what the purpose of the dog is.

"He's a working bomb dog," one of the men says. "I'm taking him back to my compound."

They examine the papers, they examine the dog, they examine the man's face more closely.

○

You pace back and forth as fear shadows you like a stalker.

○

A Triple Canopy motorcade moves along the six-mile Road of Death to Baghdad International Airport at eighty miles per hour. The vehicles contain David Mack, Lava in a crate, people being taken to the airport, and Triple Canopy gunmen in bulletproof vests who point their weapons out of cracked doors and windows to keep other drivers from getting too close.

The vehicles zoom as a pack around slower vehicles, up onto the shoulder, and into oncoming traffic when necessary. Twelve people were killed by roadside bombs on this highway in the last month. They move as fast as they can.

○

Move on, the pamphlets tell you. Get some sleep, your friends say. You take vitamins, you ride your bike forty to fifty miles every day, you floss regularly, and none of it obliterates the faces or the missing parts or the eyes of stray dogs you left behind in the desert. The ones you never touched.

Stop feeling sorry for yourself. Do not operate heavy machinery. In case of accidental overdose, call 911 immediately.

○

The first thing Brad Ridenour sees when he steps off the plane is David Mack and Lava on the tarmac by a Bongo truck loaded with gear. Brad's lost so much weight, though, David doesn't recognize him.

○

And then the e-mail arrives. But instead of opening it, you sit there and stare at the computer. You think about things like whether you'd ever blow yourself up for your country and whether you'd feel better about things in general if you did.

No, you decide, you'd only feel dead.

○

"So this is Lava," Brad says.

"This is Lava," David says.

○

Then you open it.

○

Iraq closes its border with Jordan. Four Romanian journalists are kidnapped in Baghdad. A major US newspaper reports that "mental disorders" among Afghanistan and Iraq veterans are on the rise.

○

Then you read it.

○

Car bombs kill eleven more in Baghdad.

○

"As of 1600 hours Iraq time, Lava is out of the country . . ."

○

Twenty US troops are wounded at the Abu Ghraib prison attack.

○

And for the second time in your adult life, you break down and cry.

CHAPTER THIRTY-FOUR

April 2005

THE STORY OF how Lava made it back was covered in the media, but some of the details are mine alone.

Brad Ridenour flew with two other Vohne Liche dog handlers to Amman, Jordan, where they passed through customs without any questions. They spent the night in one of the few hotels in Amman that allowed dogs, but because the dogs had to be stashed in an underground parking garage the hotel didn't use for parking anymore (to minimize the threat of car bombs), Brad spent most of the night down there.

Brad's dog, Vischa, was seven years old and the mother of several litters, so she didn't have much patience for the adolescent puppy with the weird collar and bad manners who wanted to play all the time. She was elite. She was Bomb Dog. She had orders she knew how to follow and a decent collar on top of it. As Lava bounced around and pulled on her ears and nipped at her ankles, she flattened her ears and gave Brad the eye: *Where did this little pain in the ass come from?*

In the morning the dog handlers were dropped off at Royal Jordanian, where extra-special fancy fees, magic fees, popped up like mushrooms after rain. First they were detained in a small room for some time where fees were demanded for allowing the dogs into the airport. Then they moved on to customs, where more fees were demanded for allowing the dogs to leave the country. By the time they boarded the plane for Chicago, there wasn't much cash left among them.

○

Ken Licklider made his flight in time and landed at O'Hare. There he hooked up in the terminal with John Van Zante and Kris Parlett, who'd arrived the night before.

Standing with John and Kris were a reporter and cameraman for ABC's *Good Morning America*, which would later show footage of Ken, John, and Kris greeting Brad Ridenour at the gate, then of the three guys waiting in the baggage area, and then of John's face kind of scrunching up as Lava's crate rolled through. Later, John would explain: "He comes up on this conveyer belt along with all of the other baggage, and that's when the dam just broke, when we saw that crate."

I'm thankful they didn't get some of the rest on film or at least thought best not to air it. Like John trying to find out if Lava spoke English or Arabic; like John rushing Lava outside and then exclaiming, "His first pee on American soil!"; like Lava's behavior once he got to the hotel room, which was described by John and confirmed by Kris as "Running and running and running around the room. In circles. Bouncing off the walls. Wow."; or like my face when John finally called me in California and said: "He's here, buddy. He's safe now. He's an *American* dog."

○

I should have applied for an Academy Award for my performance the next day when John and Lava flew into San Diego and yours truly, surrounded by several dozen reporters, photographers, and camera operators, waited at the Helen Woodward Animal Center in Rancho Santa Fe for them to arrive.

Personally, I didn't like the media there. I felt awkward, like I was supposed to be saying and doing things that were beyond me. But John Van Zante and the center deserved this for all they'd done for Lava and me, and if the story brought more attention to their mission, then it was the rock-bottom least I could do.

As we waited for the van from the airport to arrive, reporters stood around me in a semicircle asking questions:

"Colonel, when is the last time you saw your dog?"

"About two months ago, I guess."

"Were you ever in any danger as you tried to rescue Lava?"

"Me? No. Others, though . . ."

"Can you describe what you're feeling right now?"

"Feeling? Uh . . ."

"What would you tell people who might suggest your time would have been better spent saving people instead of a dog?"

I stayed cool. I smiled. My face, as blank as Oscar's, betrayed nothing. There was really nothing to betray, because during the entire time I was in Iraq, I tried like hell not to think too much about it, and now at the crucial moment, when it all had to come together in front of the public and *mean* something that wouldn't embarrass John Van Zante and the center, I had nothing to say.

I stared off into middle distance and tried to look like I was fashioning my profound answer in some profound way, but the only thing I could come up with for those who might question my time management in Iraq was that we're not supposed to save anybody, it's not our job, and if it was, we'd be shipping peace activists by the boatload over there to try to talk the insurgents into liking us.

But you can't say that out loud and receive applause.

Besides, Lava wasn't a little Iraqi kid the guys found alone when they stormed the compound, and I mean, come on, does anyone really think we would have just left a little kid there to die? If Lava had been a child, he would have been scooped up, given desserts from a dozen MREs, handed off to some nice person in the Red Cross, and bang, the Lava Dogs would have been instant, just-add-hot-water heroes, exactly the way we Americans like them.

Instead he was a mangy little mutt, and I have to explain that while we Americans want heroes with clean underwear and want swelling music to accompany the word WAR! as it rises up on the screen with our boys whistling the national anthem in the background as they march through grain fields in France, it's not that way. It never was, and it never will be.

Luckily, before I have to answer the question, the van from the airport with Lava pulls up.

I can see his face through the window and see how big he's gotten in the last two months, but it's the same face, the same goofy look in his eyes, the same crazy tongue hanging out sideways, and I hear cameras click behind me and wonder how I'm supposed to act at a time like this.

I sure as hell am not going to get choked up, so when Lava hops out of the van, stops and stares at the reporters, then turns his gaze toward me, I look a little above his head so I don't see the recognition cross his face, don't see past and future connect in his eyes, don't see Annie, don't see Matt, don't see the little wienie asleep with his nose in my boot, because if I do, if I see any of it, I'll lose it then and there, and none of my comrades in the United States Marine Corps will ever speak to me again.

The next thing I do see is Lava headed my way. Fast. In that run of his he has trouble breaking. I bend down to deflect the crash, and that's when I see it, the look in his eye that no one else sees, only it's not a look that results from missing me or being lonely or being scared.

The look in Lava's eyes as he bounds toward me as fast as his legs will carry him is an older version of the look he gave me when I first stomped my boot at him in the compound; an evolution of the look he gave me when I entered the Lava Dogs' building and he peed in submission; Part II of the pathetic, pleading, *please-don't-do-this* look he gave me when I betrayed him at the Jordanian border by shoving him back into the mean driver's crate.

And what's it saying that nobody but me can see?

I am going to kick your ass.

Film footage later shows a dog barreling toward a well-composed Marine in uniform who bends down, catches the dog in mid-leap, stands up and turns circles with his face buried in the dog's fur, and all you have to do is add hot water, and bang, instant answer to the question.

Why wasn't my time spent helping people instead of a puppy? I don't know, and I don't care, but at least I saved *something*.

EPILOGUE

THE PUBLICITY WAS good for the Helen Woodward Animal Center. John tells me that as a result of Lava's part in the Home 4 the Holidays drive, thousands of orphaned animals got homes that year.

About a month after we got back, John Van Zante received an interesting letter in the mail, which I look at from time to time. It was dated May 5, 2005, and responded to the letter John sent to one of the California senators back in February:

Dear Mr. Van Zante:

Thank you for your request for assistance with a federal agency. Please be assured that your matter will receive serious attention, and that I will make every effort, consistent with federal law and ethics standards, to assist you. However, I will need to have your written consent on file before I can open a formal inquiry into your case.

Therefore, please send your written and signed request for assistance to [address]. In your statement, please include your name, your address, your phone number, any relevant identification numbers such as your social security or alien registration number, a brief description of your case, and your signature.

Once again, thank you for writing.

Annie ended up flying back to the States after her trip to Cairo, where she spent time refueling with her husband and their dogs. Soon, however, she was off reporting corruption and scandal in Russia. We still stay in touch, and I still worry about her, because now she's back in Baghdad again.

Matt Hammond flew back to the States, where he spent a long time recuperating from the multiple surgeries performed on his back and legs. We both work at Camp Pendleton now and even have dinner together once in a while. He's fully recovered from his wounds and says he wants to go back to Iraq for another tour.

Ken Licklider went back to Indiana, where the kennel flourishes. It is now the largest trainer of explosives detection, police service, cadaver, and narcotics dogs in the United States, and if you're tough, brave, honest, and love dogs, give Ken a call; he can still use some help.

I don't know what happened to everyone else, like the surviving Lava Dogs or Sam or the Iraqi soldiers I trained, but I think about them all the time. I want them to know that. I hear it's been tough . . .

As for Lava, he's happy, I think. He's got a new collar and eats only expensive dog food these days. We climb mountains and roam the beach and sit in outdoor cafés on the waterfront and watch the waves and the people pass by. He's made some four-legged friends in the park who don't know how to play soccer, but that makes him exotic and cool.

Lava is still the product of his upbringing, though. He can't sit quietly for any length of time, eats everything and then throws up, jumps at loud noises, and protects me from threats only he understands. Like we'll be driving down the road and pass some guy on the sidewalk who's minding his own business, but something about him gets Lava to thinking about Iraq, I guess, like maybe the way he walks or the way he's dressed, and Lava goes absolutely, certifiably, straight-to-the-moon-and-back *wild*. Only he's not bouncing up and down and *rooing* these days. He's not even just barking at a stranger like a regular dog. He's in full devil-dog attack mode, lunging and gnashing his teeth and getting so worked up as he tries to get through the window that he gets lost in that zone no one, not even me, can access.

Lava has been through *several* obedience classes and is making progress but has yet to graduate from one. That's okay, though. I'm pretty much in the same boat in more ways than one, and we keep each other company as things straighten out.

Besides, I figure he's still paying me back for what I did at the Jordanian border.

We have a new family now, Lava and me. On the summer solstice in June 2006, in a private ceremony on Catalina Island, I married the most wonderful woman I've ever known. She and her son have a dog about the same age and size as Lava, along with a cat and a white rat. The animals are all best friends and Lava's taken to protecting my stepson in much the same way he protected me in Iraq—he sleeps with him every night.

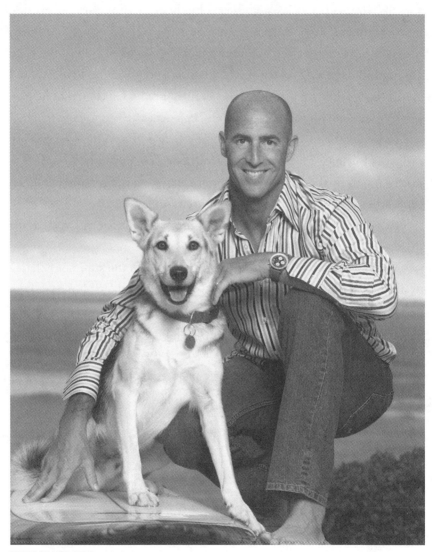

PHOTO BY LORI STOLL

CHAPTER THIRTY-FIVE

WHAT CAN I tell you about Lava and me back home in those early wonderful, crazy, unsettling days?

That the rambunctious puppy I rescued and brought to California saved me? Check. That he sheltered me from some unexpected assaults when I needed his help but didn't know it? Check. That we were partners and friends, members of a mutual and exclusive support group? Check. That we were strangers in a strange land? Abso-friggin'-lutely.

The California I'd left in September 2004 didn't feel even remotely the same to me in April 2005. Little had changed, but everything had changed from my perspective. The people I was closest to looked at me differently; treated me differently, as though I was fragile and would break on contact. Many just avoided me. Maybe it was me who changed more than California had.

Lava full grown looked more like a small husky than anything else—fifty muscular pounds of raw and agitated nerve endings with large, expressive eyes, a thick coat, and an active tail. He never seemed happier than when he was on the move, which was basically always. He ate up life like he attacked the leftovers I'd feed him from the dinner table—voraciously, hungrily, gratefully.

At rest, a rare event I must admit, he was beautiful, almost serene, asleep and curled up on the floor, breathing contentedly. He was the sort of dog people passing by would always ask, "What kind of a dog is he?" And then in the next breath, "He's a beautiful animal."

Yeah, I'd think, he's the kind of dog you'd write a book about.

Look into a dog's eyes and you'll see life and love and understanding in a mute poetry that tells you everything will be OK. Lava had such a knowing, intelligent look of confidence. That's what Lava did to me—for me. And I did the same for him. When I think about those first days back from Iraq, it was Lava and me, me and Lava. Whatever I did, he was there. Whatever decisions I made, he was included. We were a single unit, a fire team, battle buddies. As Forrest Gump said, we went "together like peas and carrots."

My efforts getting Lava out of Iraq were returned a hundredfold. If I were inclined to somehow calculate the benefits against the challenges and stress—not to mention the violations of General Order 1A—of bringing him to California, the ledger would lean heavily toward doing it again and again and again, enduring the same aggravating tension-filled, nearly soul-crushing effort to get him out.

But you can't do an accounting of such things without a lot of second-guessing, and I'm not inclined toward that sort of introspection anyway—at least I wasn't back then. Besides, it doesn't work that way with a dog. Certainly not with Lava, who did everything unconditionally—just like the way he came into my life in Fallujah. In California he lived as if he knew every day away from the bombs and the insurgents and the death was a gift. I wish I'd had his ability to accept this gift, but it's not as simple as it would seem. At least not if you're a reasonably well-adjusted adult human being and not a dog whose greatest worry is when the next bowl of kibble is coming your way.

It is not a simple calculus, having a dog, loving a dog. It's not a checklist you can fill out and carry in your hip pocket, as you do with mission orders and tactical objectives. Looking back at it now from the very good place I am in fourteen years later, Lava overwhelmed me. He was innocent and guileless and ballsy and faux fierce and, at times, out of control. Back in the States I realized quickly he didn't care where he was, as long as he was with me. That was all that mattered. The feeling was mutual.

In California Lava chose his comforts—sleeping with my stepson Sean, running in a park, chasing a ball or a stick. His exuberance did not fade. How could it? He had an energy, a certain magnetism, that sucked in everyone. And I was the biggest sucker of them all.

Lava did not choose his demons. Neither did I. That's the way it goes . . . you don't get to choose your demons. They just show up when they want—largely based on your experiences—and they were there for both of us, in multitudes. Fallujah had assured us of that. Lava and I faced our demons together because that was how we worked. As I said, we were a team. The chaos of Fallujah couldn't be shrugged off like a bad dream. Any combat veteran knows that, whether they admit it or not. And anyone who hasn't been in combat—and maybe they're the lucky ones—will never understand. The stress, suffering, anguish, loss, and, well, the shit, cannot be duplicated in a laboratory or by watching a movie. Neither can love. Especially the love for someone who's been with you through the stress, suffering, anguish, loss, and shit of combat.

As crazy as it sounds, even to this day, Lava and I spoke a language no one else heard. A lazy wash of wagging tail against my leg, deep and contented breaths as he slept at my feet, a slight cock of the head as an ear jumps to attention. Maybe a Lava head butt to tell me to get up and start paying attention to him.

I got it and so did he.

In California Lava lived as he had when he entered my life in Fallujah—exuberant and feisty and, yes, challenging.

Take the first time I met Pam and her son, Sean. I was petrified becasue Lava had just grabbed Sean's arm in his mouth and dragged him down to the ground in a La Jolla park. I have to say, that frightening moment worked out well, though it scared the shit out of me at first.

Jesus. I loved that dog.

As we settled back into California, Lava and I let it out. We lived — we survived Fallujah, Lava and I, and we made the most of it.

So how did it go, getting back to California? Man, it was a hell of a trip, but more about that later.

Today things are better than ever. I have a great career and I'm surrounded by people who love me and care about me. Coming back to California I thought I had put my battles behind me. But I had one more to fight. And Lava was with me the whole way.

In a way, he's with me still.

You'll see.

CHAPTER THIRTY-SIX

As I STOOD at the rail watching Catalina slowly fade into the horizon, and became lulled by the gentle Pacific roll on the way back to Dana Point, I thought about this.

It's 7,600 miles from Fallujah to Santa Catalina Island, an inviting gem off the Southern California coast. That's easy enough to figure out. What was more difficult for me that afternoon was how I could gauge the distance between then and now. Between Fallujah fourteen months earlier and where I was at this very moment. I couldn't use a GPS to lay out the exact distance. That would have been like trying to measure the distance between heaven and hell. I'm not sure I was equipped with what I needed to see that distance.

The ferry headed southeast in a soothing, hypnotic roll in the gentle swells. The sea scents and salt air and sun were perfect. The weekend had been amazing. Heading back, I was on top of the world. I was a married man with a family.

I thought: I have an astoundingly beautiful, caring, and sexy wife and an almost eight-year-old, very energetic son. I've been surrounded for two days by friends and a great calming joy. Everything was right with the world.

Lava had started the whole thing in a very Lava-like fashion.

It was a familiar pattern, like following an old script. That's how it was in those days with Lava back in the States. We were at the park in La Jolla where we often went to let Lava blow off his considerable steam. I'd been chatting with another dog owner and caught a Lava blur out of the corner of my eye. Shit.

First came panic as I saw him streak toward a young kid then knock him over. Out of control again, Lava had somehow determined the kid wanted to play.

Double-shit.

As I ran the thirty yards over to the two of them grappling on the grass, I imagined lawsuits and Lava getting locked up, and bans from the park where we often played. When I got to the boy, I saw that he was fine, smiling in fact, though he certainly must have had a jolt—this bullet dog coming at him like a crazed wolf heading for its prey. My heart rate dropped quickly. I checked for damage. Was the kid bleeding? In shock? Did Lava tear his shirt? The only evidence that anything strange had happened was Lava's slobber on the boy's arm.

Then I noticed the mother, who'd just run—very powerfully I have to say—twenty yards in about two seconds. She'd seen the whole thing unfold, terrorized I guess, but unable to stop it because the always determined Lava wasted no time doing what he wanted to do.

Seconds later, as I pulled Lava aside and watched the kid stand and shake it off, I had the great serendipitous realization that the boy belonged to the beautiful woman I'd seen at the park. I noticed her months before and saw her often, but had never exchanged more than a casual hello and smile—you know, the local dog-park smiles people exchange because they're there for the dog, not because the place is a hot dating scene.

The mother. Yes. The woman I had been staring at for months. The fit, tan, gorgeous woman with the Lab mix who seemed to be at the park with her son and dog nearly as often as Lava and I.

By then, Lava and I had been back in the States long enough to have settled into a routine. We were on the same frequency, like we could read each other's minds. But as acutely as we were attuned to each other, he could not have known how much I wanted to say more than "Hello, how are you?" to that woman.

Or did he?

I had once commented on an Ironman sweatshirt she was wearing.

"Do you do triathlons?" I had asked expectantly, as if that piercing question would open a long and interesting conversation.

"Not triathlons; open-water outrigger canoeing," she said as she ran off to pull her dog, Koda, back onto the grass.

She was not being rude, or cute. She was being a dog owner at a dog park.

But Lava attacking her son?

Yeah, that was better than "Do you do triathlons?"

Meet the love of your life at the dog park? Really? It sounds crazy, like a strained and cheesy plot from an old movie, but there it was.

Lava's over-the-top, hell-bent hello did what I had been trying to do for weeks. It put Pam and me within talking distance, and once we both calmed down and saw Sean, her son, was fine, we laughed it off and parted in a pleasant way. At least we were past the frozen-smiled "Hi, how are you?" stage. Lava also made his acquaintance with Koda, Pam's dog. The gears were slowly meshing, the ice melted by Lava's wacky greeting.

Not that Lava's surprise attack was an instant karmic connection, but I hoped something was there as I walked away. I felt something click.

I saw Pam over the next few weeks and we'd say hi, smile, and chaperone the dogs, but there never seemed to be a chance to sit down and talk. There were just too many park interferences.

A couple of weeks later I was at the park with Lava early one Sunday morning. The usual crowd had not yet trickled in, to paraphrase Billy Joel. It was quiet. Perfect in fact, the sun warm and the day ahead promising. As I sat there watching Lava and planning my Sunday following a morning surf, I thought, "What would make it better would be for Pam to show up, now, before the distractions set in. It would be the perfect time to finally talk with her."

I really did think that.

To continue the strained Hollywood plot, as I tossed Lava a few sticks, I looked up and saw Koda, then Pam, silhouetted against the rising sun, an outline of perfection, heading toward me.

Pam was fit and lean and muscular and beautiful. She happened to be wearing her Ironman sweatshirt, flip-flops, and a short white skirt. She moved sensually and gracefully, like the athlete she was. My heart nearly exploded.

She walked over slowly, said hello, and sat on a stone wall next to me while we watched Lava and Koda play.

We talked easily and relaxed, without pretensions. Neither of us felt the need to impress. We were comfortable in our own skins and skipped the usual bullshit ballet of first-time connections. We had nothing to be phony about, no need to be anything but ourselves. I'm not a big fan of phonies or posers, to put it mildly. Neither was Pam. That was instantly refreshing. We drifted in and out of the easy conversation without artifice. There were long gaps of silence during that first conversation, but neither of us felt the need to fill them—the silence enveloped us rather than driving a wedge between us. That whole first lengthy conversation—we must have talked for close to an hour, though neither of us was paying attention to the time—was charged, like a slow and steady electric current was taking over.

At one point the talk lulled. We sat and watched Lava and Koda chasing each other in circles.

Then I got nervous as hell. You'd think a naval aviator with one hundred carrier landings under his belt, a Marine with multiple parachute jumps who survived ground combat in Fallujah, would be cool as the other side of the pillow under any circumstances. I hemmed and hawed a bit; I cleared my throat.

The moment of truth.

"Would you ever think about having a drink or something sometime?"

"I'd like that," she said.

"Great," I said.

"I can get a babysitter tonight," she added.

Sonofabitch, I thought. Not that I was any kind of a playboy, but I actually had another date already planned that night, not expecting the answer I got. This, my friends, is a classic example of being on the horns of a dilemma—a super-cute girl roughly half my age who would be good for my ego on the one hand, and a lovely, winsome beauty on the other. It took me about half a New York second to abandon Plan A because Plan B was so much more appealing.

That night Pam and I had a great Mexican dinner, after which I suggested a nightcap at a different Mexican restaurant down the street. I was friends with the owner, and the bartenders looked at me as some sort of local hero. They even had a photo of me from Iraq in the very large display case at the entrance to the restaurant.

All that interested Pam but it didn't impress her. I liked that.

We had margaritas, our talk slow and easy, then walked slowly back to my car and I drove her home.

When I pulled up to her place, I parked and walked her to the front door. I had imagined the moment. Who wouldn't?

I kissed her as we stood on her front steps.

The reality was far different than my dream. It was soft and magic and sensual. It was welcoming and promising. It was everything I had been missing for longer than I cared to admit.

That was a beginning that continued to Catalina Island June 2006, when Pam and I were married in front of Sean and family and friends who had made the trip out to celebrate the glorious event.

Pam and I had gotten to know each other very well by then. We'd surfed and spent countless days having a breakfast burrito and coffee afterward. We talked about books and films and passions and our pasts. Pam never asked about what I had done in Iraq, or the things I had seen. I offered nothing. I had no interest in talking about Iraq and what I had done and seen.

The wedding was nothing short of spectacular. Outside, a few cumulus clouds dotted the horizon as they scudded over the Pacific. It seemed that day we could see forever. And the wildflowers of Catalina, flame azaleas, mountain laurels, and purple lupines were blooming in a colorful explosion. This was galaxies away from those other explosions that had been such a daily part of my life, back when.

I was not in Fallujah. It was truly a hallelujah moment, glorious and expectant.

My friend Eric and I had earlier rented a small boat and taken Sean fishing. He caught a shark and we all laughed about his great good fortune—not even eight at the time, and he caught a shark. It was a great moment.

Lava stayed home with a dog sitter and I did not mind. But he was on my mind as I stood at the rail on the hour-long trip back to Dana Point, contented and exhilarated and, I guess, at peace.

I was a married man with a family and I was winding up my career in the Marines. Prospects rose ahead. I was ecstatic about everything: for the future, for Pam, for Sean, for Lava, for life.

My family is everything in the world to me.

Earlier, we had agreed to rent our La Jolla beach cottage, a three-bedroom, two-bath beauty just four short blocks from the beach. It seemed like a terrific way to start our marriage, with some serious money from people willing to spend a fortune for the location.

As the summer progressed, Pam, Sean, Koda, and Cheddar the cat went to Idaho to spend the summer at the family house overlooking Hayden Lake, and Lava and I rented the granny flat in a friend's house. I felt like a displaced person by the end of the summer, the good idea of renting out our house long since faded.

It was an odd way to start a marriage, I thought. The room in the house was a bit irritating. There had been other things that had been irritating me, too. I couldn't put my finger on the reason why.

I was in love, I thought, and love conquers all.

Or so they said.

CHAPTER THIRTY-SEVEN

MY FRIENDS AND other Marines—especially then-Major General Dennis Hejlik, who wanted me to help him stand up the Marine Corps Special Operations Command (MARSOC)—most likely thought I was crazy when I said I was retiring. He probably thought it was like watching someone slam on the brakes while he was rounding third and heading home, a rash decision when my career trajectory was heading upward. To this day, Denny chides me when we speak, the first words out of his mouth being, "You should have come with me to MARSOC, Colonel!"

No doubt, Denny calling me "Colonel" is more of the jab he's taking, because I retired as a lieutenant colonel. I would have more than likely retired a pay grade higher had I heeded his request and moved to North Carolina those many years ago.

I never did anything rashly. Acting without thinking in combat does not end well. I enjoyed the challenge of change. I certainly had never fretted about change. I've always been comfortable with my decisions and with the adrenaline that often went along with doing something more challenging and different.

I'd taken some risks, getting Lava back to the States being one of them, but I'd always found the benefits outweighed the risks.

When I decided to retire from the Marine Corps I'd been in the military for twenty-one years—most of my adult life. I'd admassed one-hundred arrested landings on aircraft carriers as a naval aviator, jumped out of perfectly good airplanes numerous times, and I'd been to Iraq where I danced on the razor-sharp edge between life and death every day. I'd seen the world—its beauty and the depravity of its inhabitants.

It was a tough decision, but I knew it was time for a change. I was ready for something new. I had no regrets about it either, about anything I had done. And I never looked back, a useless exercise. George Washington said that "we should not look back unless it is to derive useful lessons from past errors. . . ."

One of my last assignments at Camp Pendleton—"the West Coast's Premier Expeditionary Training Base"—was as senior watch officer, the first point of contact for Marines deployed worldwide. If a Marine fell overboard on a ship in the Med or got hurt in Kandahar or in trouble in Iraq, the first calls were to the watch officer. I had to find answers, quickly. I'd have to decide at three in the morning what the next step would be—including whether to wake a sleeping general and let him know. It could be tense and it was not without its challenges, but compared with Fallujah it was a walk in the park.

Lava didn't care what I was doing as long as it was with him. We continued our Dynamic Duo routine, even to the point where I took him to work at Camp Pendleton and let him into the combat operations center—or COC—after everyone went home. Totally against regulations, of course, but Lava was with me because I had chosen to make a very rare exception to the rules to get him where he was. With me, away from Fallujah. You don't get to be a lieutenant colonel in the Marine Corps by bucking the system—usually.

Lava didn't care what I did. I'd let him sleep in my Land Rover then bring him in later while I worked the 2000 to 0800 (8 p.m. to 8 a.m.) watch officer shift. He'd pad into the COC, find a place to curl up under the desk where I worked, and go back to sleep. I'd check on him and smile. Then whisk him away back to the car before 6 a.m. so that no one was the wiser. That is, of course, until the one night when Lava snuck out of the COC and took a shit in one of the colonels' offices. That "movement" garnered huge laughs from everyone, except the offended colonel (sorry, Racer, wherever you are).

Looking at it now, my experiences in Fallujah were becoming a slowly growing chancre—ugly and festering and persistent. What I'd seen and done there stuck to me in a way that nothing else had, and I couldn't seem to shake it, though I tried to bury it. Back in the States after Fallujah, things were not moving as smoothly as I thought they would. Back in California everything—my longtime friends, familiar places, the old sights and smells that had once been so comforting— all seemed off, like they were in another dimension.

Lava was my one haven.

Still, if anyone asked, I'd say all is well, everything is fine. No issues.

My watch officer assignment did have its benefits. I had time to cycle with a group of hard-charging bicycle racers immediately following my night shift, and surf and spend time with Pam, whom I was seeing regularly. There were distant promises on the horizon.

Deciding to retire was just a continuation of what I'd been doing since I graduated from high school in a Pittsburgh suburb and headed to the University of Miami, a big move. After college I left an easy gig teaching high school and coaching football in Tampa to join the navy and learn to fly airplanes. Six years in, I transferred from the navy to the Marine Corps. I thrived on change, I guess, and felt stifled by the sameness of everyday life in some fashion.

So as far as retiring from the Marine Corps, it was time.

That's the thing about change. You have to see the possibilities ahead and not be tied to the comforts of the past. I knew it was time to leave Pittsburgh, which was in the middle of a harsh transformation itself. The steel mills were closing and the city was having a bit of an identity crisis.

I had grown up comfortably in a mildly affluent suburb. We were not suffering like many area families as the mills closed and laid off thousands. My dad was successful and my parents always support-ive, if tough with the discipline. I did okay in school. I did have one thing in common with kids from the area though—football. It's tough to explain football in southwest Pennsylvania to anyone who hasn't been part of it. Fans are rabid and fanatic and at the time, the Steelers were close to unbeatable and offered hope to the 'Burgh when there wasn't much else.

Still, I didn't see Pittsburgh in my future.

I walked onto the football team at Miami as a defensive back and made the team, though I never really played. Those were the days when Miami football was beginning to make a name for itself. My first coach was Lou Saban, a "distant cousin" of Nick. Later I played a bit for Howard Schnellenberger. Our quarterback at that time was Jim Kelly, another Pennsylvania kid. I don't want to get carried away here with my tales of athletic glory. I was a blocking dummy for the most part, but still I was not afraid to give it a shot—and I did make the team in the spring of my freshman year, relegated to punt and kickoff coverage, and punt return special teams. And then came the first knee injury.

My first job in the real world was in sales, but that wasn't me. Besides, who's gonna buy anything from a twenty-two-year-old know-nothing? I certainly wouldn't have.

After knocking around a bit, I took up teaching math at a Tampa high school and serving as an assistant coach for its football team. My biggest challenge was overcoming my youthful mien, or, baby face. I still looked like I was eighteen or nineteen and apparently some of my students developed crushes. I had to meet with the principal to dispel rumors that I was some kind of hot date for the clearly underage high school students who bragged to their friends that I had taken them out. Fortunately, I had been friends with the principal's son during our years at "The U," where he had been a baseball player. Otherwise, things could have gotten dicey.

While I enjoyed the teaching and coaching — I've always enjoyed being able to help others — I wanted something more challenging and visited a Tampa navy recruiter, took some tests and was intrigued to learn I had the right stuff to become a certified naval aviator, something I'd never before considered. The officer-and-gentleman allure, and the challenge of making it through the intensive training ahead (especially when told how unlikely it was I'd make it) appealed to me. Well, I made it, was commissioned an ensign in the US Navy, and was in time conducting carrier landings and traveling the world.

I loved it.

When my six-year navy obligation was up — they don't send you though all the training without getting their money's worth — I was hooked on the military life. It was a little less predictable than teaching math but the adrenaline highs made up for it. I did not get the same jolt from explaining the nuances of the quadratic equation to a roomful of kids who, let's face it, were not exactly on the edges of their seats.

During my time at Aviation Officer Candidate School (AOCS, the one made famous in the movie *An Officer and a Gentleman*) I was supremely impressed by our Marine Corps drill instructor. There was something about the way he carried himself and acted. He impressed me, and there was more to it than his whole no-bullshit attitude. He had an aura. Marines don't whine and they get it done. And they are proud as hell. I liked that. I was in awe of the guy, to tell you the truth.

The Marine Corps is much smaller than the other service branches because its training can be soul-crushing and physically exhausting, designed to produce the best and eliminate those who can't cut it. Its *esprit de corps* — its morale and pride and sense of self and mission — is much stronger and more steeped in tradition than it is in the other services. Marines eat up their exclusivity and flaunt it. Why not? Marines do things no one else does. And besides, we have, by far, the best-looking uniforms!

As my commitment in the navy was drawing to a close, I did an inter-service transfer to the Marine Corps. I woke up that morning as a navy lieutenant, and by 1500 that afternoon I was a Marine Corps captain. From that point forward I immersed myself in the Corps values of honor, courage, and commitment.

I traveled the world in the Marines and ate it up. I had done two tours in Iraq. I had made my way up the ranks. I had the general's invitation to make the Marines a career for at least a few more years, and I certainly would have been promoted.

But back home in California after Fallujah, sitting at my desk in Camp Pendleton, Lava at my feet, Pam on my mind, certainly, I decided it was time to retire, to do something different.

I loved the idea of it all. I loved the idea of change. Change was good.

It still is.

CHAPTER THIRTY-EIGHT

THAT FIRST ALL-MEXICAN (burritos and margaritas) evening with Pam—the easiness of the conversation and the electricity, the magnetism—changed everything. After that first night, free of the idle dog-park chatting, time passed quickly as I thought about our plans for the next day or the next week. That allowed me to set aside the unease I'd been feeling since I'd been back, the odd disconnectedness.

We were hungry in those days to get out, to get to know each other, to impress each other. We'd talk, and we'd share the small details of our lives, the things that had brought us to where we were and who we were.

I kept busy at Pendleton—Marines being Marines, there were hot spots all around the world—but I have to say, the all-night watch officer hours suited me—and Lava.

We were in California after all, and with Pam and me being active and energetic, we spent most of the time getting to know each other outside.

We surfed as much as possible, grabbing our boards and heading to the beach every chance we got. At one point I'd bet we surfed nearly every day for a month. Pam was completing a doctoral program in anthropology. She didn't push too hard to learn what made me tick, to study the undercurrents of where I was at the time. I was not unhappy about that. I was still processing Fallujah, trying to shake off what I'd seen and done. I thought I was doing a good job of it, that all I needed was more time and distance. I wasn't into staring too directly at the past. I wasn't into talking about it either, with Pam or anyone else. A few cocktail party conversations with my neighbors warned me of the glaring gaps in their understanding of what was going on in Iraq, and of their total lack of sensitivity. Headless bodies in the streets and bloody firefights didn't blend well with the latest news on La Jolla real estate values or the difficulties of carpooling kids to soccer games and concerts. I'll take a wild guess and say that talking about dogs eating the dead would have stopped most conversations.

So Pam and I would talk and surf and move and soak up the sun and each other. We'd take turns introducing each other to our favorite post-surfing meals—fish tacos and egg, potato, bacon, and cheese burritos.

Pam was into long-distance outrigger canoeing, an intense Hawaiian import where crews paddle in open-ocean races for forty miles or more. I loved long rides on my bike. Neither of these activities lent themselves to fun and frolic with Lava and Koda. Before Pam, I did nothing without Lava. I needed the comfort he brought, and his companionship. Our shared journey had bonded us. Having Pam in my life altered my relationship with Lava, but it also showed me how much he had given me, and everyone else in Iraq, where simply petting him reminded us that we were still human beings.

I didn't depend on Lava the same way after I met Pam.

But he was still as loyal to me as he could be and our reunions after I had gone on a ride or spent the day with Pam at the beach were joyful, as if I'd been away for years. Lava didn't hold grudges.

Lava was holding onto something though.

The first time I heard it, I was startled. It began as low, keening, warning notes that Lava had uncovered some buried, aching discomfort. Those first mournful notes grew into an unsettling wail, a howl that sent the hair on the back of my neck to attention. It was eerie, chilling. A lot of things startled me in those days—a car door slamming or an unexpected tap on my shoulder—but there was nothing like Lava's howl. He would let it fly for no reason at all.

That howl was a great release of some hidden pain Lava could not escape or erase.

More than anything it was almost paralyzing in its sadness. I could not do a thing to rid him of that, and it wasn't for lack of trying on my part. I didn't know it then, but Lava's baleful cries foreshadowed my own future cries for help.

CHAPTER THIRTY-NINE

MY GOOD FORTUNE in surviving Fallujah, of heading into retirement after a long and rising career, of meeting Pam and looking ahead to a promising future did not make the hells I had been pushing away disappear.

Still, I thought, things were going well. I was a lucky man.

Marines don't equivocate, they act. They lead from the front and take responsibility. No hand-wringing, no doubts. That's how I was trained and how I acted, and it had worked well for me.

A minute of carelessness one afternoon would make me question everything—my efforts to bring Lava out, my sense of self, my pride. It would make me wonder what it was all about, what it meant.

If I were on the streets in Fallujah, my senses would have been hyperalert to anything that was off, that did not seem right. Smells, odd movements, no movements where there should have been, someone's stare, a passerby's jumpiness. It pays to be psychic in combat, especially in fighting where calm might be bad, chaos normal, and death can come from any angle and any person. Nothing is what it seems and anything can happen.

But I was in California, home—safe, quiet, and predictable. No one did anything unexpected. Days in SoCal were always blandly predictable.

One sunny pleasant afternoon, back when Lava and I were living in the effete neighborhood of Rancho Santa Fe, we headed out from the house, about to take a walk, for God's sake. I was in my civvies, civilian clothes, and I was going to walk my dog. How normal is that? It was the sort of normal moment I had daydreamed about in Fallujah while I was struggling to get Lava out and back to California.

By then Lava had dodged mortars, escaped General Order 1-A, and survived suicide bombers, a night flight to Jordan to avoid surface-to-air missiles, and a lot of other things that should have killed him. Really, what could happen on a beautiful day on a tree-lined street in the refined confines of Rancho Santa Fe?

I hadn't put the leash on Lava as we stepped out. A few strides into the walk I noticed the increasing pitch of an engine that did not match what was supposed to be a twenty-five-mile-an hour speed limit. I see a black SUV—not the sort of SUV you'd see in Iraq, armored and dirty and dented from tough daily demands, but new and no doubt freshly waxed. The driver, a woman, was doing close to forty or forty-five though the peaceful neighborhood.

Lava was in front of me, standing on the curb. He turned his head to see where I was, as if to say, hurry up, let's go.

Lava was still skittish. He might have understood how to survive in Fallujah but he had no idea about rules of the road and life in California. I froze at the sound of the car, then began approaching Lava cautiously to not spook him. I needed to get a leash on him, quickly.

I glanced up at the approaching driver and the SUV. A dog on the curb and a man inching up to her. Certainly she must have seen Lava and me. She didn't slow down.

Lava bolted into the street, wanting only to get moving and have me with him. He was oblivious to the SUV. I can still hear the screaming brakes and smell the acrid burning rubber from the driver's feeble last-minute efforts to stop.

If I saw the impact, I have blotted it from memory. I can still hear Lava's high-pitched cries of violent injury, shock, and fear. I had heard the howls of wounded men. They could, in no way, compare to this. It was bloodcurdling. He was hurt and no doubt badly, but Lava being Lava, he got up and bolted for our front door. I didn't stick around to check on the driver and didn't care. I needed to find Lava.

I followed the trail of blood back to our house, running through the trees barefoot as I'd abandoned my flip-flops, knowing I needed to get help quickly. When I found Lava on the front steps, I caught a glimpse of exposed bones and tendons. His belly and his tail had been stripped of fur from being dragged beneath the SUV.

I was overwhelmed with grief, tempered by anger that I could have been so stupid. Looking at him—so damaged, so hurt, so vulnerable lying on my front step—turned me upside down. I had done so much, and others had done so much, to save this little war mongrel, and now I had fucked it up immensely.

How could I have let this happen?

I had made it through some terrible shit in Iraq, endured unspeakable things that were light years from this pleasant RSF street. Was this neatly coiffed, SUV-driving woman in a hurry going to be the one to bring me to my knees?

She nearly did. Lava was still breathing and looking hopefully into my eyes. There was still a chance, but that careless driver and my own momentary stupidity came so fucking close to doing me in.

When I picked him up to rush him to the hospital, I knew that. I could feel it. I knew also as I laid Lava in the back seat of my Land Rover, as he looked up into my eyes, that I meant the world to him. That he had already forgiven me. I knew then what he meant to me as well.

Rushing to the hospital, I promised him this would never happen again.

Lava is a fighter.

It took three long days to know Lava would survive. He was determined and he kept fighting, through several operations and a lot of painful rehab. If I could have, I would have undergone all the surgery and the stitches and the rehab myself, without anesthesia. I wanted to feel Lava's pain.

He hobbled on three legs for weeks as he slowly healed. I would, for those same weeks and long after, question how I could have been so careless and stupid.

Even limping and barely able to walk, Lava still wanted to play, to chase things and get into trouble. There were too many things to do and places to go, even as he was dragging his damaged leg in a cast. I spent eight thousand dollars to get Lava back to being Lava. I would have spent everything I had and borrowed more.

The whole horrible scene, the frantic, panicked, airless trip to the hospital and the days that followed, reminded me of why Lava had come into my life and why I had brought him to California. It was the same reason the young Lava Dogs had saved him in the first place.

Lava was a daily reminder that I could love again. That life mattered.

CHAPTER FORTY

LAVA WAS NOT the only thing I brought back home.

I was not aware at first that I had more than clothes in my baggage. I wasn't alone. Thousands of returning vets were doing the same thing at the time. But I believed with the fervor of a newly baptized evangelist that none of my experiences in Iraq had affected me in the long run.

It turned out that I was one of more than a half million returning veterans carrying unseen wounds.

Lava was, too.

Iraq had offered up a weird alphabet soup of insidious things that would kill you—RPGs, IEDs, VBIEDs (vehicle-borne improvised explosive device), UXO (unexploded ordnance). As the casualties mounted, at home, at peace, far from combat, this condition would quickly be tagged with another acronym, PTSD, post-traumatic stress disorder. Later called the unseen wounds of war, nearly all—if not all—returning combat veterans were afflicted with at least a modicum of this horrible condition.

Lava and I were among the walking wounded. We were uncounted in those early days, because I didn't think I had a problem. I denied it to myself, first and foremost, then to everyone around me. People wondered about me. My closest friends didn't believe me when I said I was fine.

I was better than fine, I thought.

Back home I saw a lot of returning veterans drinking their faces off every chance they had. I now know and recognize that getting drunk or high allows a vet who can't shake what he did or saw in Helmand Province or Fallujah to escape the overbearing feeling that he no longer fits in back home. I'd had that feeling—a vague other-ness that nothing seemed right anymore—almost from the minute I'd stepped off the plane from the Middle East that final time at March Air Reserve Base in Riverside County.

I wasn't into the excessive drinking, and getting high was a non-starter, especially while on active duty. Instead I became a difficult guy to be around while I tried to sweat out my demons with heavy exercise—intense bike rides, exhilarating double black diamond ski runs, surfing, and motorcycle riding. I would get on my Suzuki GSX-R 1000 (pronounced "Gixxer") and race up Interstate 5 to Camp Pendleton at a head-whipping, tear-inducing 135 mph, with no regard for my own life, and little regard for those on the highway around me. One little mistake, one overcorrected speed wobble, and I would be the proverbial smear on the highway. Now *this* was living!

I started to focus on what I had determined was the privilege and entitlement of some of the people I'd run into—a smug Star-bucks barista or one of the many self-important assholes who dotted (no, littered) the streets, restaurants, and my orbit as I tried to live my life in Rancho Santa Fe and La Jolla. If I had to hear one more person brag about little Billy (who was typically a whiny little shit) or complain about their wine cellar not regulating the temperature properly I was gonna smash them in the face and let the chips fall where they may.

I'd think: What had they done to deserve such a high regard for themselves while some nineteen- or twenty-year-old kid spent six months or more in the worst urban combat the Marine Corps had seen since the battle of Hue City in Vietnam more than forty years before? I'm sipping a coffee—just a plain coffee, nothing special—in one of the local coffee shops trying to shake images of beheaded bodies and rotting corpses and the permeating odor of burning excrement, and everyone around me is lost in their own worlds. Like there was nothing more important than their upcoming manicure or private trainer session (which they more often than not *really* needed). That grated on me. No, it pissed me right the fuck off.

I was not alone. Lava was suffering too, and he articulated that pain in many different ways. I clung to Lava. Lava was hope and life and all that was good and normal. That's why we were inseparable.

Years back I'd adopted a mantra about things: don't stick around if it's not fun. That's why I left Pittsburgh for school in Miami; why I left teaching for the navy; and the navy for the Marine Corps.

Iraq was not fun and I planned to leave it behind. Forget about it and move on with my life.

But PTSD was not something I could close the door on. It wasn't something I could eliminate by simply denying it was there. I couldn't will it to disappear, try though I did.

The interminable wars in Iraq and Afghanistan, brutal and violent and unpredictable, were beginning to produce a wrenching by-product. Combat veterans were coming home with toxic baggage they could not let go of, could not deal with. The chaotic way wars were fought there—unexpected strikes coming from nowhere, roadside bombs, urban warfare, intensive street fighting, nerve-shredding house clearing, long and dangerous missions inside enemy territory where snipers can hit you at any time—can very quickly put unimaginable stress on a soldier or Marine.

The effects of combat stress probably go back to the first time someone picked up a rock and threw it at a caveman neighbor who was pissing him off. What we now call PTSD has been called many things in recent wars — "soldier's heart" in the Civil War; "shell shock" in World War I; "battle fatigue" in World War II; and "post-Vietnam syndrome" for the long struggle there. Returning veterans from each of those conflicts required psychological care for the delayed effects of their exposure to combat.

Call it whatever you want, but the effects are sinister. Returning veterans can't stow away the terrors and the fear they lived through. They can't just neatly move back into daily life. For many vets, coming home meant alcohol and drug abuse and violence and broken relationships and suicide.

One study by M. J. Friedman from 2006 lays it out clearly, if clinically: "PTSD symptoms [are] typified by numbing, evasion, hypervigilance, and re-experiencing of disturbing incidents via flashbacks. Veterans and other non-combatant participants in war who have outlived traumatic experiences typically suffer from PTSD."

I could not close the door.

Some mornings I'd wake up covered in sweat, my sheets soaked, and have no idea where I was. It would take a few minutes to shake it off and realize I was safe at home. It was a hell of a way to start the day.

TV shows could set me off, especially if I was watching a news report or a documentary about the war. If the screen showed an image I'd experienced, say an explosion or a firefight in the street with bodies strewn everywhere, I'd freeze, every nerve taut. Of course, that was a natural reaction — that sort of thing has to affect anyone, no matter how tough they think they are. If you had held the hand of a young Marine who had nearly died in an IED blast, you'd remember. These things are uniquely impactful, and you are affected — unless you're some kind of sociopath going in, and I wasn't . . . I hope.

The worst thing for me in Iraq, and I imagine everyone else who experienced it, was the unnerving sound of incoming mortar and rocket fire. You couldn't do a single thing about it but take it. Sure, you could look for cover, but by the time you'd find it, it was generally too late. Perhaps the worst of it was that there was no release, no enemy to shoot back at. It's a totally helpless feeling, sitting, waiting, and hoping nothing hits within a radius close enough to kill or, worse, maim.

Back home, for no reason, I became jumpy as hell, something I had never experienced. But after Fallujah I'd jump during suspenseful scenes in movies. In the middle of a safe and quiet movie theater. I had never experienced this before. It was an unsettling development.

Attending a Marine's funeral I flinched noticeably when the honor guard fired off a volley of M-16s before taps. I knew it was coming and I knew when, but I came close to jumping out of my shoes. I couldn't control it. Think about the absurdity of that one—a twenty-year combat veteran jumping at the sound of gunfire that he knew was harmless and knew was coming.

The others at the funeral might have seen the honor guard paying a final tribute. I saw body parts in the street.

These things gnawed at me. Had I somehow become a coward?

Trying to escape, I did intensely physical things most people would shy away from. I surfed big waves that many others would watch from the beach. I skied as many steep double black diamond, neck-breaking, mogul-strewn runs as I could, and went back up for more. I'd take huge, aggressive risks during bike races and waterskiing or wakeboarding. Routine was boring, I needed to take chances.

I did those things for fun, though, and while I was on top of a wave or passing a rider on a sharp downhill curve, I still knew someone was not about to blow my head off. I was not waiting, even in those hairy moments, for the bullet that would take me to my own sweet Valhalla.

Trying to avoid it, or distract myself from it was not working for me. I would explode at the slightest provocation, especially if I was caught off guard.

One pleasant, warm evening, coming back from an intense indoor training session with my cycling teammates, I was pulling my car into our driveway when another car came barreling down our one-way street in the wrong direction—way too fast. It happened all the time. Somebody too lazy to drive around the block. We had a lot of kids in our street—Sean included—who would not be looking in the right direction.

I pulled in front of the guy to block him, planning to have a little talk with him for being a dickhead. He saw me and pulled into a driveway in front of me. I didn't recognize him, and thought he'd get out and walk into the house. Instead he whipped his car back out of the driveway, turned around, and sped out of the neighborhood.

He's a lucky man, but I was steaming.

While I was busy trying to ignore the "new" me and my new world, I always had Lava.

Lava was pure, sweet joy to be with. He was an escape. He was always as happy to see me as I was him. Lava seemed to have an unshakable belief in living. He was a survivor and his craziness, his antics, eased the anxieties I'd accumulated in Iraq. We both were experiencing unspoken, unarticulated, choking fears that grew from living moment to moment in Iraq as if each day, each breath might be your last—of never being sure of what would happen next, and knowing full well that if something unusual was about to take place, chances are it would not be good.

My own new world of tension and apartness and irritation was, of course, straining relationships, but it was not breaking them. People around me—Pam and Sean, my friends, Marines I worked with and my cycling partners—all gave me space and time while I struggled to keep things under control and search for answers.

Lava was enveloped in his own crisis, as much a victim of what he had seen and done as I was. Like me, he had his own way of dealing with it. I began to notice that the neatly kept yards of La

Jolla seemed as dangerous and unpredictable to Lava as any street in Fallujah.

He would become frantic at the sound of a UPS truck rumbling down the street. He'd howl like a mad wolf when anyone came to the door, especially if they rang the doorbell. He seemed to take a certain ferocious pride in defending my family. Lava would protect us with his life if need be. He would sleep contentedly every night curled up in bed with Sean, but awake and out in the world he was always on guard; always, it seemed, ready to spring at a perceived enemy. He played excitedly with Koda, without a trace of aggression. Out in the world I had to be on constant guard, though. Lava would get into anything, and he was clueless about the danger.

He had his own quirks, and God knows what they were about.

One afternoon playing at the park, he ran by a couple eating pleasantly on a blanket spread out in the early afternoon sun. Lava stopped, turned, walked calmly back onto the blanket and peed all over it, behind their backs. We made ourselves scarce before they noticed. Was it embarrassing? Sure. Funny? Definitely.

Still, for the most part, Lava was exuberant and his enthusiasm spilled over onto everyone. He could make people smile. He loved going on long runs with Pam or playing in the park with Sean and me.

Still, there was something hard to pin down about Lava, and I could not eliminate it with training sessions or, for a while, meds to calm him. Lava was terrified of the ocean, his whole body would shake at the sound of pounding waves, his feet uneasy in the shifting sand. Did that bring back memories of Fallujah? Did the waves sound like bombs?

One Christmas, before we were married, Pam had driven out to Gardnerville, Nevada, where we planned to spend the holidays with her family. I got a sitter for Lava and flew out the next day. When I landed in Reno I had a frantic message. Something had set Lava off and he would not stop howling. He was going full-nuts crazy and howling like he was being eaten. Even worse, he wouldn't let the dog sitter near his kennel, and when she did try to open it at one point, he bit her. I called Graham Bloem, Lava's terrific trainer. Graham could get Lava to listen without raising his voice. I asked Graham to get Lava and keep him calm until I got back.

Lava—and I—needed help.

Anyone in the military will tell you it is a fate worse than death to admit weakness, and most will go to any length to avoid going to medical. We were trained to fight, not to hide behind a medical diagnosis or, God forbid, talk to a therapist.

I reluctantly accepted I could not control things the way I had done my entire life. It was getting to be too much; as a Marine officer I had been trained to make decisions. I had tried to fight it in my own way, on my own terms, as I always had, like it was a war I could win. I knew it had nothing to do with courage or weakness or toughness. This thing was hurting me and everyone in my circle, everyone around me: Pam and Sean and my new son, Mattox. They would all need me—and all of me.

I would get help. When I thought about picking up the phone to make a call to say I might need therapy, I felt nauseated. As if I had failed.

I wanted to do some research, to learn what was out there to help. I made some phone calls and talked to therapists and learned as much as I could, thinking maybe I'd write about it. Maybe help others with what I'd learned. *From Baghdad, With Love* had given me a platform. At that point though, I was still convinced that though many other vets needed help, I didn't.

Lava would need some too. I was just not sure where to find it.

CHAPTER FORTY-ONE

My DECISION TO get help for myself—finally—didn't slap me awake with a Paul-on-the-road to Damascus epiphany. I wasn't suddenly struck dumb by the obviousness that I should ask for help. It took time to get there—and a lot of thought. I mulled over options, questioning my motives, my strength, what I was doing, and what I thought would happen.

Slow awakenings have an edge over capricious decisions. They have more of a solid base that won't erode as quickly.

Still, picking up the phone was one of the toughest things I'd done. In a way I was still fighting it, still thinking I could just bull my way through.

Therapy? Are you fucking kidding me?

I had been trained to fight, not to whine to a therapist or to talk to a complete stranger about my unease. As I said before, most military guys will do anything to avoid going to medical. For most it's a stigma they'll never erase.

By the time I made my call I had other things that were more important to me than my career, which by this time was over. I'd officially retired as of 1 February 2007, just one week following the birth of my son, Mattox. I now had a loving family who were concerned about me, and that included a new son who would be looking to me for advice. I had friends who were worried. They didn't understand what had happened in Iraq, but they knew something was off, that I was not the same guy who'd left them.

I was not thrilled about the thought of being "in the system" but I knew I wasn't alone. PTSD had become epidemic among returning veterans.

I still clung to the idea that I just needed a bit more time to clear my head, but not as tenaciously as I did at first. I had no physical symptoms. I was fit as hell, actually—racing bikes competitively, skiing, surfing—taking care of myself. I wasn't overwhelmed by panic attacks. I didn't suddenly keel over when surprised. I didn't soil my pants because some guy honked at me when I crossed the street the wrong way.

But I knew that my agitation and temper and explosiveness and general jumpiness had put Pam and Sean and a lot of other people on edge. That was not what I wanted. When I made the call, our son Mattox was four months old. Would he grow up being afraid to ask me questions?

In Fallujah—quite naturally—I had real fears. My mind would race before combat, organizing the countless details I'd needed to manage to keep everyone alive. Coming down from that is not easy and at times it seemed like I didn't have an off switch.

In rare moments of rest I'd think about the mortars, and the IEDs, and the snipers, and I'd wonder if I'd ever see the ocean again. I wondered if I'd have my head blown off. I'd think about the possibility of returning home without a leg or an arm, or with a brain injury, which I was diagnosed as having years later. That I'd need help eating and pulling on my pants.

I wondered if I would ever have a chance to sit down and have a cigar with my best friend, Eric, or surf, or go out for a long ride on my bike. I thought about my parents and how they would feel if they lost their son. Not pleasant thoughts, I know, but that was my reality and the reality of many other vets. Those thoughts become toxic, like a slowly growing cancer.

When I got back I bottled those toxins up.

In the Marines, I had learned that the only way to conquer fear is to confront it. Stare it in the face and remind myself that I was stronger than anything I faced. When I picked up the phone to make an appointment to talk to someone, I knew I needed help to confront this one. The balance had shifted. I wasn't going to steamroll my way through this, crushing it.

I had a responsibility to my loved ones to be a good husband and father and friend. I'd been swimming upstream far too long. Survival at home is just as critical and uncertain as it is in a combat zone.

I owed it to Lava, too. He was my partner and we shared so much no one else could understand. He had given me so much.

I diluted my distaste for stepping into what for me had always been a recourse for the weak by telling myself that with what I learned, I could help other vets. In a way it was a continuation of how I had always been. As a kid on the playground I couldn't stand to see kids being bullied and I always jumped in, fists flying, to help.

By the time I picked up the phone, *From Baghdad, With Love* had struck a chord with readers and in short order it became a *New York Times* and international bestseller. The response was astounding. This gave me what marketing people call "a platform." I had an audience who wanted to hear what I had to say.

I'm not one to spend too much time patting myself on the back, but this was good news. It seemed like everyone wanted to talk to me. I sat for newspaper and radio interviews. I was featured in a piece on the CBS Evening News. I did a book-signing at a convention of publishers and booksellers that had a line that stretched hundreds of yards. Groups sought me out to speak to their members. And I got paid to do it.

The attention allowed me to address the issue of returning vets and it provided me with a nationwide audience who wanted to listen.

I thought if I could learn more about treatment for suffering vets I could help them. Maybe I could help myself along the way.

It was a win-win.

Still, I had preconceptions about therapy and had steeled myself. I wasn't sure how I'd react the first time someone would ask me, "How does that make you feel?"

Well, let me tell you. Yeah, I'm a bit angry. I saw some horrible things and I'm trying to deal with them. People with a sense of entitlement or undeserved self-importance piss me the fuck off. Is that wrong? Is that unjustified? Jesus. Give me a break.

I exaggerate only slightly when I pictured the therapist asking me, as I lay on a couch, if my third-grade teacher had forced me to wash the chalkboard—or some part of her—after class and that I had never been the same since. I figured the therapist would be handing out meds like candy. Have some Prozac. Try this Xanax, please. You can never have enough Xanax. I pictured myself walking around like a zombie, an emotionless robot.

Chemical solutions didn't appeal to me. "Jay's over whatever was bothering him about the war. Too bad about the new personality, though. He fell asleep at lunch with his head in the soup bowl."

One stark statistic shows I was not alone. It took me more than a month to get in to even begin discussing setting up appointments to talk to someone.

The whole time I waffled over whether to get help, Lava was dealing with his own stresses—and they were not unlike mine. Lava was overprotective and tended to go berserk at the UPS guy, or sometimes at the slightest provocation. He startled easily. He would become aggressive, especially if he thought anyone was threatening me or Pam, Sean, or Mattox.

Despite his edginess, Lava still had the same enticingly wonderful personality that gave Matt Hammond—so severely wounded in Iraq—the time to recover and get back into the fight. Lava had something that gave Matt hope. Back in California Lava was doing the same thing for me.

Lava knew who mattered. He had his own hierarchy of who was important — like he was a bouncer at a hot new club that people were fighting to enter. Only so many people could get into Lava's world. That would become very clear after Mattox was born.

A friend from the dog park had broken into Lava's inner circle and Lava would greet him like a long-lost friend when they saw one another. They'd play enthusiastically. One afternoon I was pushing Mattox in a stroller, Lava padding alongside, just moseying along, not a care in the world. My friend saw us and crossed the street to get a look at the new baby. Two feet from the stroller, Lava was on him in an instant. It was scary, ominous. No real harm — if you don't consider torn up fingers and a couple of arm punctures real harm — but it was clear that Lava would protect Mattox at all costs.

I was quicker to find Lava help than I was for myself. I took him to countless training sessions and his veterinarian, Bruce Lindsey, understood and gave me meds for Lava that helped to smooth his natural tendencies — the ones bred in the midst of the chaos in Fallujah. Those would not go away. It wasn't as if Lava could talk to someone about it. Meds for Lava sort of helped him, but mostly eased my own angst over what he was experiencing. I kept him moving, too, and busy. I tried to avoid surprises for him, and had him eating right and getting enough rest and exercise.

Still telling myself I was doing research to help other vets, I picked up the phone and made a call.

At first, all I did was see a psychiatrist at the VA medical center in La Jolla. She asked the typical questions: Did I have thoughts of hurting myself or others? Did I have nightmares (shit, I was sleeping all of three hours a night so there's no dreaming because there's no REM sleep, and she's the one who went to med school)? — the usual. But rather than ask me the real, hard questions, she prescribed a couple of medications—citalopram, a selective serotonin reuptake inhibitor (it's what keeps you from having Tourette's-like outbursts and/or punching people in the face because they pissed you off and you can) and trazodone for sleep.

My "research" took some time before I dropped the pretenses and started therapy in earnest for myself in 2014. I learned a lot. Counseling did not offer an instant solution. It had taken me a while to get into the woods, and it would take a while to get back out. But I dropped my preconceptions and I opened my mind.

And I talked—to professionals who had experience dealing with this growing national problem. They were experts who were on the cutting edge of reducing the problems tied so tightly to PTSD. God knows they had a large pool of candidates—men and women returning from combat—to work with.

When I finally opened myself up, counseling helped me immensely. But it would be too late, and at the expense of my marriage. Still, as they say, better late than never, while there was still hope not to destroy all my relationships.

I learned to talk about my emotions because Lava had shown me that part of my personal integrity is to be true to my feelings. That mongrel war dog had won my heart and mind, and he was an important part of my life. He'd shown me that my feelings exist, that they can't be pushed away into a corner. Fear exists; anger exists; sadness exists. Lava's friendship and the love of my family helped to alleviate the intensity, but the emotion was there under the surface. I continue to work to make sure there is some release from time to time. Part of that is simply allowing myself to have those feelings.

I grew and I learned—that I needed to keep busy, that I needed to focus on the future, not the past. That the Marine Corps might have turned me into an efficient killing machine, but it had not taken my heart.

I knew also I had to find a way to keep Lava's demons at bay.

CHAPTER FORTY-TWO

TIIC DOG PARK SPARK that ignited us wasn't so much extinguished as slowly smothered by the detritus of daily life. For Pam and me—mostly me—the small details and minor irritations every couple faces became larger than they should have. I can see that now. The great exciting color we began with turned slowly gray as small disagreements became large, and silent disappointments found their voice.

It didn't help that I was still dealing with the PTSD, which caused explosions that threw off their own domestic shrapnel just from simple disagreements most people would shrug off. When our skirmishes began, I had not yet started counseling, and the medications seemed to be no more effective than a placebo, though they'd not had enough time to firmly grasp my medulla oblongata or frontal cortex, or whatever part of the human brain is supposed to be repaired (impaired?) by selective serotonin reuptake inhibitors, or SSRIs.

By the time I started to learn how to deal with the tension and the aftereffects of Fallujah, we had gone too far down the wrong road. Little things became bigger; big things became immovable obstacles.

The immutable law of inertia applies to relationships, I learned. Once things began heading in the wrong direction, it became difficult to pull it back, though we tried. Fighting to save the marriage was just another battle I was immersed in. We couldn't seem to find common ground. It began over the small things, some of which I now readily admit I could have—should have—controlled better. That's the irony of it all, I suppose. I needed peace and instead I found more battles. I just wasn't equipped to find that peace . . . yet it was staring me right in the face in my loving family.

I needed order, more than anything. I had lived my life in an orderly fashion. A half-open kitchen cabinet door or a jutting counter drawer would annoy me. An unloaded dishwasher—or one that was loaded, in my thinking, incorrectly—would set me off. In the Marines I would have reprimanded such untidiness. I was retired, sure, but as they say, once a Marine, always a Marine. Petty? Yes, of course. I know that now.

Therapy was frankly unsettling. I opened myself up to a complete stranger and answered questions even Lava knew better than to ask me. Still, I did it for myself, for my family, and for my fellow Marines. I wanted to let them know *h-e-l-p* was not a four-letter word. I learned quite a bit about the collective psyches of our military units, and later—too late—I learned about Pam and me and the fact that survival at home is just as critical and uncertain as it is in the combat zone.

With us, those small irritations exposed tender areas and left raw nerves on the surface. These are the vulnerable things we usually bury. Reactions are amplified and overreactions common. Small things seemed big; big things seemed unconquerable.

Still, even in those uneasy times, my stepson Sean was growing into a wonderful young man and I was immensely proud and thankful to have him in my life. Even in the middle of the skirmishes he excelled at soccer and lacrosse, did very well in school, and became the type of son other parents wished their children emulated.

Mattox was a gift I never thought existed. He was unconditional love at first sight—something I didn't know was real until he arrived. When I held him, everything else in the world vanished. It was just the two of us. My worries and cares evaporated. I wanted only to protect him and provide him with a happy and healthy life. I wanted to become a better father and man for him to look up to. I wanted to be the example that would help him become a thoughtful and trusted leader, friend, and father in his own right.

I had not made a career out of failing and for the longest time I was determined not to when it came to these precious things. But children add complications and soon enough Pam and I were overwhelmed by philosophical differences over discipline, among other things. Our bond had not fused solidly enough to withstand the fracking pressures. I'd grown up with loving but firm parents and an environment where my obligations as a kid were clear. There was no ambiguity. I wanted the same for Sean and Mattox.

As the battle lines were drawn, each of us picked up allies. My friends knew I was a solid and unshakable guy. Pam's friends saw me in caricature—the tough, hardened combat-scarred Marine insensitive to the nuances of daily life in California. Allies formed and the no-man's-land between us widened. It built over the years.

Lava, though, remained a constant. He didn't take sides. He continued his contagious exuberance, though I was starting to worry that even the meds could not calm his terrors.

Admittedly, I made some mistakes. But as they say, there are two sides to every story. I needed a sense of order after the chaos. I needed things to be done in a certain way. I wanted Pam to know that and make some accommodations until I found some peace.

Pam's friends told her I was a jerk and she believed them. And, if truth be told, I often was a jerk.

In December 2014 Pam and I were summoned by child welfare services to answer charges that Mattox was in harm's way. Someone had decided that I was overly aggressive. Did they hear him crying? Did they see him alone and neglected? I'm not sure who it was, but things could not be further from the truth. I still have no idea who filed the complaint. Come in and talk to us, the notice demanded. Pam and Mattox and I were all interviewed. Friends and neighbors came to my defense and the matter was put to rest, but the horse was out of the barn. We were on the list.

By then I was sleeping on the couch most nights. On a Saturday night in March 2015, around 10, Pam dropped the big one.

"You have to leave. I need my space."

After so much confusion and misunderstanding, that was pretty clear to me.

I threw some clothes into a backpack and headed for the hills over La Jolla, where I slept in my car for two nights, stunned that I'd just been asked to leave the house, confused, and not sure what the future would bring.

Friends going out of town offered me their couch for a week, and then another friend offered up the same granny flat in her house that Lava and I had shared back in the summer of 2006, for a month until I found a place to live in downtown San Diego. Lava, meanwhile, remained in La Jolla, in the comfort of the family he'd come to know and love. Pam and I agreed to keep talking, hoping for a solution.

In September, I found a therapist at the VA in San Diego who would work with us and enrolled us in a couples counseling program that offered a year of talks. At our first session I talked openly of the mistakes I had made. As we finished, the counselor gave us each a detailed questionnaire to be completed, separately, and brought back with us the following week.

As we were leaving Pam offered a glimmer of hope when she thanked me for my openness and for arranging the session. We headed back to our own places.

She called me the next day.

"I don't want to go back."

"Why?"

"I don't like the questionnaire. I find some of the questions to be inappropriate."

Quite frankly, I was taken aback. Unless there was something to hide, there should not have been anything inappropriate about this at all.

"I understand," I said, though I clearly didn't, "and we don't have to go back to the VA.

"But look, I did the legwork and got us into a year's worth of counseling, so now it's going to be up to you to find the new counselor. I'll go to whomever you want, but you've got to find the person."

She said she would, but it never happened. I guess it was too little, too late. I was crestfallen. I was still in love with Pam at this point, despite the difficulties, and would always care about her. After all, she is the mother of our children, and no amount of fighting or differences between us will ever change that.

CHAPTER FORTY-THREE

THE RESULTS OF a test during a routine physical at first seemed to me to be karmic overkill. If I were still playing football it would have been like some sort of cosmic piling-on penalty. Pam had thrown me out and Lava's unease was increasing. I was living away from my family, seeing Mattox only occasionally, and just becoming settled in a new position that was taking up as much of my limited intellect as I could spare. Was there anything else waiting to make me feel shittier? I knew one thing that could—whining about it. I would not go there.

My physician, scanning a sheet of paper, looked at me calmly and said, "I don't like these numbers." When I glanced at her computer screen I saw that my A1C—indication of diabetes—was visible. "You think I have diabetes?"

"Oh, sorry, wrong screen. Your PSA is 11.4."

I was surprised.

"That's gotta be a false positive. Can we set up another blood draw?"

A week later, nothing changed. In fact, it got worse—marginally, but still worse. My doctor called with the results.

"It's 11.5."

I was stunned.

One of the worst things about these sorts of medical dramas is waiting for the next test. Medical things have their own schedules and sometimes it might feel as if the delays in getting answers are designed to inject the maximum amount of anxiety to ponder your fate.

"You might have prostate cancer. We'll know in a few weeks after the next rounds of tests, which, by the way, will include a digital rectal exam."

The results of that intrusion were less ambiguous.

"Your prostate is enlarged by at least 50 percent. We need to biopsy."

I had been in worse situations. It wasn't as if I'd step out the door of the doctor's office and wonder if I'd be alive at the end of the day.

I began a series of the most intimate probes of my nether regions—jabbing and inserting while I lay on a table in the flimsiest of hospital gowns, knees pulled into my chest—and surrendered all pretenses of privacy and dignity. By then I had shaken free of the questioning and surprise. I adopted a "let's get this over with and move on" attitude.

In the course of the various exams, there was one common and assured result. Blood, and lots of it. The day of the biopsy I had to get a tetanus shot and another shot of some antibiotic (due to the expected bleeding that occurs from a biopsy). I'd been overdue for the tetanus anyway and I took that as a good development. Positive thinking in these situations is crucial.

The biopsy procedure is not for the faint of heart or for the prudish. I lay on a table on my side in a fetal position—the "target" exposed for all to see. The technician applied lubrication for the moment of truth delivered by something that looked like it was designed to make anyone reveal their deepest secrets—a spring-loaded probe inserted to capture small core samples of my prostate. I listened for the trigger pull, waiting for the moment of impact. It felt like someone had pulled back a thick rubber band and snapped it against my prostate.

You get the picture.

It was not fun, but still I took some small comfort in learning that the investigation stopped after twelve cores. Some guys get more than twenty. This of course came with the doctor's casual admonition that I'd be bleeding from the most sensitive of orifices for some time to come. I was not disappointed. Had I not been informed, I'd have rushed to the nearest emergency room after the first urination following the procedure. Instead, I stood in rapt horror looking into the toilet as what could only be a blood clot passed through my urethra. This was beginning to make the *Halloween* movies look like rom-coms.

The results, when they came in, were predictable. I had prostate cancer. I began to plan my assault on this thing as carefully as I did any mission in Fallujah.

I thought about the options, and there were many, and turned to friends for support and advice. I found all I needed.

I looked briefly into getting treatment through the VA but quickly rejected it after one doctor there seemed overly enthusiastic about operating quickly. I had no need for scalpel-happy surgeons when complications included, among other things, incontinence and worse, impotence.

A dear friend had been diagnosed with prostate cancer only six months before. He was a bright, deliberate guy, a wealthy man who could get the best treatment available anywhere he chose. He never did anything rashly and considered all factors before deciding.

I called him.

"Look, I hope you know how much I admire you and try to emulate you in all that I do," I said. "In fact, I admire you so much that I've decided to get prostate cancer too."

He told me that after months of flying around the country talking to experts, he had found a consulting group in Los Angeles that recommended Scripps Proton Therapy Center (now, California Protons) in the San Diego suburb of Mira Mesa. Proton therapy offered the benefit of being treated with substantially lower doses of focused radiation controlled to stop at the tumor, not blasting away at neighboring organs in the process. For prostate cancer, the targeted proton beam can avoid radiation exposure to the bladder, rectum, and small intestine.

That sounded good to me and I met with Dr. Carl Rossi to arrange for treatment. Pam went with me, which was reassuring in a way. I started on January 4, 2016. By then, I had decided to make the best of it. So many other people were facing much more dire situations, getting treatment that at best might add a few more months, much of it painfully, to their lives. I considered this to be "baby" cancer, not the real stuff that requires months of chemotherapy and radiation.

I had a lot more I wanted to do and felt assured I'd still have the time to do it.

Sill, when treatment begins with flimsy gowns and rectal balloons, there is only so much one can do to keep a positive attitude — and your self-respect.

The folks who do the actual work of giving patients their treatments have a difficult job of staying upbeat for their patients, and I was just trying to help lighten their loads, if even a little bit. One afternoon I put on a pink women's gown and welcomed the staff to "Feelin' Feminine Friday," which sparked some rare smiles. Another day I grabbed a marker and drew a line above my crotch, adding "NO PEEKING" so that the gal who did my bladder ultrasounds before the treatments could get a chuckle. Later I drew targets where the 'pencil beam' enters my body and added "Radiation Here." In a small way I added an unusual sound in these often sad, quiet rooms . . . laughter.

I finished treatment on February 11, 2016. It was a humbling and at times humiliating and tiring experience, but I'm grateful.

All is well.

CHAPTER FORTY-FOUR

THE FINAL DECISION, wrapped in a terrible truth, was both a blessing and a curse.

I had saved Lava—we had saved each other—and it was becoming clearer that I alone would have to make the decision to free him from the terrors he never quite got over. As heart-wrenching as the decision was, I knew it would be a final act of kindness for all he had done for me.

I thought for years that my time in Fallujah was the worst in my life, but I was wrong.

I returned one evening to our condo in San Diego, next to Petco Park, where the San Diego Padres play, to what looked like the aftermath of a car bombing. There was debris everywhere. Lava had somehow scratched out and eaten part of a wall. There was drywall dust and chunks of sheetrock everywhere. When he'd had his fill of sheetrock and drywall he started in on a door jamb.

I thought that living in a secure building in a downtown high-rise would make a difference for him, and for a time it did. He would still get his bark on, but not as often because there were fewer irritants to cause him to become upset, and he would calm down and listen better. He didn't seem as stressed out. But that relief was only temporary. Lava was once again becoming increasingly ill at ease. He just couldn't stop.

I called the vet and described the scene.

"It's time," he said.

I knew but I said nothing.

"You've done more for Lava than anyone would have," he said. "You gave him eight years more than I ever would have expected. There's nothing more you can do."

I was sick at heart, but I knew the vet was right. I knew others would have given up years before. Lava had given me hope and restored my faith in life itself. I owed him that.

The inevitable saying goodbye—knowing it was time to free Lava from his demons—had always been there, hovering as his unease increased. I knew this final act would end his constant agitations. I knew it would in some small way repay the debt I owed him for all he had done for me. I knew it would be a tribute in some dark way—a final heartbreaking measure of love.

I knew all that, but grief is not an abstraction. Even though I was prepared, I still felt as if I'd been blindsided. I was aware in some fashion that the circle of life—the beginning, middle, and end we all face—had not been broken that day. It was completed with Lava's last sigh.

I told myself that as I walked from the vet's on January 4, 2016.

I knew all that but I didn't feel it. I felt nothing. I was numb. I was gutted.

The sadness of anyone who has ever lost a pet is a wrenching, terrible inevitability that can be avoided only if you give up breathing or live in a self-involved vacuum. It is paralyzing. Lava had been a force in my life for years. That same day I was due to start my radiation therapy, but that was the furthest thing from my mind. At first there was a certain numbness, which I suppose was good. I'd get up, plod through the day, and try not to think, try not to find myself catching my breath at an invading memory. To this day, I have to force back the tears with a lump in my throat as I write about this most heartbreaking moment of my life. It's on a par with the day I learned my father had died.

That would settle. I was fortunate that my life and Lava's had intersected. I would later develop a tender gratitude. We all should live life with Lava's immediacy and rambunctiousness. There would be a lot more open and honest people. Those thoughts buoyed me. I could look at photos of Lava on the run, or Lava and me rolling in the grass and take comfort.

I often looked to Lava for answers. Dogs are special in that they seem to have emotions much like those of humans, but they don't seem to worry about what others think about them and their behavior. They rarely hold back. I didn't necessarily like, but was almost amused by, Lava's ability and desire to bark at anyone and everyone he saw coming by, as if to say, "Hey world, this is my territory and if you don't like it you don't have to live in it."

Lava truly enjoyed every moment of life with glee. At one point I wrote out what I saw as Lava's Rules of Life: Bark at whomever you want, whenever you want, for any reason or no reason whatsoever. Pee where the other guy (or gal) just peed. Live every day as if it is your last. You're always the smartest guy in the room if you don't compare yourself. Disobey everything you're told to do.

Lava taught me that it's how you carry yourself and what you do for others in life that really matter. He showed me that one's capacity to give—and to receive great joy in doing so—is what ultimately gives us happiness.

My advice to you is to live your life with all the gusto and pleasure of a dog. Specifically, my dog, Lava.

I have a memory that actually brings a smile when it settles in.

I can't remember clearly Lava's first moments in California. I do remember that I couldn't look at him directly as he ran toward me that sunny San Diego day. I remember I couldn't *not* make eye contact with him because Lava, well, Lava didn't let me get away with ignoring him or ignoring what he means to me.

I remember him leaping into my arms and hugging him. I remember my tears.

Lava was unconditional love. He trusted me to do the right thing. His trust gave me strength of a different sort I had never had. Having him back in my arms that day was the best thing that happened to me.

The look in Lava's eyes as I caught him mid-leap that day was pure ecstasy. When it first returned to me, I wished I could somehow freeze it forever, because that moment was the best of all the countless good moments I had with him.

Then I realize I have. That sustains me.

CHAPTER FORTY-FIVE

FIFTEEN YEARS AFTER the little wienie crawled into my sleeping bag and started an astounding romance, I've found my balance. Life is good with both my feet on the ground and knowing the ground is not a minefield of hidden surprises. Fallujah and its aftermath had made me vulnerable and left me reeling. Knowing that left a gauzy discomfort that colored everything I did. I couldn't bull my way through. The first step was seeing that; the next step—counseling—made all the difference.

I cannot stress enough to any returning vet to stop trying to fix yourself. There is help available, and as I write this, it is better and more capable and more effective than it has ever been. Nearly twenty years of war has made sure of that. You can't put a Band-Aid on gaping psychic wounds. You can't self-medicate. You are not alone. Get help, please.

Talk to someone. It works.

When I first set eyes on Lava, I had been developing thickening psychic calluses to protect myself. It was the only way I could survive Fallujah. I didn't know it then, but the first sight of Lava was the start of a decade-long effort to reconnect with the world.

Having both feet on the ground today is energizing. I still work out like a maniac, still ski and surf and fight — Muay Thai, that is. And I have taken up a new pastime, fly fishing, which has many calming benefits because you are required to devote all your focus on making sure you put your fly in the right place and watch for the telltale signs of trout about to hit your line. I have tied back in to the things that meant the most to me. I have found a balance in a way that allows me to also accept falling occasionally, to know things are not always going to be perfect. And that's fine with me. I have centered myself in whatever is happening and can remain upright. I might sway, but I never crash.

I try to follow a simple mantra: Good deeds produce good results. Good results lead to calmness, reduced stress, insight, and smooth edges.

I'm working hard now as a health-care executive. Don't get me wrong I don't float through each day like a Buddhist monk, smiling beatifically as I sit behind my desk dispensing aphorisms for a better life to my colleagues. It's hard. I get as pissed and frustrated as any executive and leader would. I do well, but it is work, not life. But work is not life.

I know that now. Jesus, it took a while.

In January 2016, ten months after Pam threw me out, I called her and asked to meet. Our marriage had headed far enough south that we were at the point where we needed to sign some paperwork heading toward a divorce.

"Are you sure this is what you want?" she asked.

I'm thinking, "You threw me out of the house, my expenses have quadrupled, I had to put down Lava, and I have cancer."

Instead, I told her, "Honestly this is the most relaxed I've felt in years. So, yes, this is what I want."

Recall, it had been three months since Pam had declared that she didn't want to go to counseling at the VA, but that she would find us another place to go. When I asked her about it she said she was still working on finding us someone—but it never happened.

That's okay though; I'm still relaxed.

Life is short. The day Lava was hit by the car in 2005 served as a sobering reminder that everything I hold near and dear can be taken away from me in the blink of an eye. It's critical for everyone to recognize those people and things that are truly important in life— those we all need to hold in the highest esteem and treat with utmost respect. Lava reinforced that for me.

I try to enjoy the simple things in life.

I eventually learned to accept the joy and happiness that come from just lying on my back in the grass while the sun's rays warm me. I learned that I could howl at the moon if I wanted to. The true measure of a man on Judgment Day is how he lived his life. I consider these things and I ask myself this question: Did I live life with dignity, modesty, and compassion for others?

I had a good run after I got back, even when I was still figuring things out. I began to ask questions of myself as I continued therapy. Have I lived a full life and shared it with others, receiving love in return? Have I found pleasure in the simple things and the wonders of nature? If at the end of the day I can answer "yes" to these questions, then I have lived a full life.

I sit here now and wonder if I'm in danger of dislocating my shoulder patting myself on the back, but even while I was clearing my head, I was determined to do what I could to make a difference.

Lava served as a focus for me. Taking me out of my memories and keeping me firmly in the present. That allowed me to build something from the lessons Professor Lava taught me. Help others, directly and indirectly. I donated portions of my book sales to charities that benefited veterans and their families. I used Lava's name recognition to bring awareness to causes I thought were important, like animal rescue and training organizations. I traveled around the country, telling Lava's story and lecturing on leadership, the war on terror, PTSD, veteran reintegration in society, and other topics. I was keen to find ways to assist veterans who suffer from PTSD and reduce the horribly increasing rates of suicide, substance abuse, and homelessness among our veterans.

At one point I was appearing frequently on both network (Fox, NBC) and local television news to discuss breaking stories, events, and issues of importance to the military and veterans. I served on the advisory board of the Virtual Reality Medical Center, a San Diego-based company with offices in Los Angeles and Palo Alto that was using simulation technologies to treat returning combat veterans suffering from PTSD.

I served as executive director of Freedom Is Not Free and became a board member of the GI Film Festival and the Rancho Santa Fe Fund. I supported the San Diego-based Challenged Athletes Foundation and raised money for Operation Rebound, dedicated to bringing sports and exercise to permanently disabled veterans and first responders.

I learned that being involved—not isolating or stewing in my dark memories—was great therapy in itself.

A colleague wrote a recommendation for me once that meant a lot and showed how far I'd come.

"Jay is a compassionate, knowledgeable, dedicated, moral and aggressive human being who has successfully contributed to our freedoms and way of life in the United States in a way that is non-comprehensible for most individuals."

That meant a lot to me.

Here's the essence of what I'd been looking for as I shook off Fallujah: it's not about work or success or how much money I make or how many medicine-ball push-ups I can do or how many black diamond runs I can make in a day—though those things matter.

What matters to me is life.

I met an astounding and understanding partner with whom I now share my life.

Felena, a successful entrepreneur and an astonishing woman, was sitting next to me at a friend's party. We hit it off immediately and, after a few months, began dating. We have been together since. Felena is an independent woman who has added depth to my life. More important, she has graced me with a peace I have not known for years.

Today, I've found my equilibrium. I no longer get upset with the small things that once drove me crazy. I'm better with everything, though I know I have a way to go.

Oh yeah. I have another dog too, Gunny, a purebred, all-black German shepherd. He's a rescue, of course. Sound familiar?

He's a wonderful, sweet, and exuberant dog. But make a wrong move near my son, Felena, or me and he'll rip your nuts off. Good dog.

Life goes on, and life is good.

ACKNOWLEDGMENTS

So WHERE DO I begin? Do I just tell you about Lava and how we came to be together, or do I thank Buck—that's my good friend, Lieutenant Colonel Ignatius "Buck" Liberto—for extending his tour in Iraq, thereby giving me the opportunity even to meet Lava? Or do I thank Colonel J. C. Coleman, the First Marine Expeditionary Force chief of staff, who "volunteered" me for duty with the Iraqi Army during the battle of Fallujah? A lot has become a blur over the year since I've returned from Iraq. After all, if Buck hadn't stayed in Iraq for six months longer than he should have, and had Colonel Coleman not recommended me as a liaison officer to the Iraqis, Lava and I would never have met. And really, that's what this story is all about. Isn't it?

Maybe the people I truly owe a debt of gratitude to are those who really rescued the mangy, flea-bitten mongrel. People like the members of our commanding general's personal security detail. Among them Sergeant Matt Hammond, who, even with his severe wounds, wouldn't let anyone near Lava if he thought they might try to harm him. Who played with Lava every day while he recovered, when he should have been in the hospital, but instead took care of the little guy. Or Anne Garrels, a brilliant journalist from National Public

Radio, who more than had her hands full trying to report the war and the elections under fire, but who always found the time and the energy to deal with a young unruly puppy, and who ultimately arranged his "parole" from Iraq. Maybe the thanks go to Sam, the Iraqi who so "doggedly" worked miracles to get Lava his international puppy passport and dog biscuits, and who took the time to teach Lava to play soccer. Sam, who couldn't come to America himself, yet did everything he could—even at the risk of his own life—to make sure Lava found a home in America. Yes, there are many to whom much is owed, especially every member of the Lava Dogs, First Battalion, Third Marines, who didn't just shoot the little guy when that would have been the most convenient and expedient way to ease their daily routines. Instead they showed that even in hell, which is what Fallujah became, it was more important to show humanity by caring for Lava when he was just a five-week-old puppy.

I need to thank all the people from Vohne Liche Kennels and Triple Canopy Security who never wavered once when they were assigned Operation Get It Done by the Helen Woodward Animal Center in San Diego. And where would Lava be without the generous offer from Iams pet foods and Kris Parlett, who paid for his trip home? I also want to thank Lava's trainer, Graham Bloem, of West Coast K9, whose gift with animals transformed a troubled pup into a fun-loving, playful, and wonderful companion. Yes, a debt of gratitude is owed to all these people.

But most importantly, we all owe a debt of gratitude to the young men and women who've made the ultimate sacrifice in the global war on terror. They have unwaveringly gone into harm's way, and promising lives have been extinguished all too soon. Since I've returned from Iraq, I've been a reluctant observer of too many memorial services for too many young Marines—many of whom were young enough to be my own sons. I say I was a reluctant participant not because I didn't want to honor those American heroes, but because

I think it's tragic that so many shining examples of all the qualities we admire in human beings—bravery, honor, integrity—and all that we hope our children will one day become, have been taken from us. It doesn't get any easier with each service. In fact, it gets harder to stay detached. I sit alone at these memorials so the young Marines who may one day go into harm's way, as I have, won't see the old gunfighter going soft. And I do it so I can retreat inside myself for reflection, knowing how sad my family would feel if it were me who didn't come home, wishing I could do something—anything—to ease the pain of those families who've lost a son, brother, father. But words won't heal the wounds. Only time heals wounds. It is my hope that some of those families will read this book and see that all is not in vain. That even in death there is hope for new life. A new life that has been given to my best friend, Lava.

George Orwell said, "People sleep peaceably in their beds at night only because rough men stand ready to do violence on their part." We all owe our thanks and gratitude to those rough men who've sacrificed so we can live in peace and safety here in America.

Last, but not least, I want to thank my coauthor, Melinda Roth, for all her hard work, dedication, and willingness to tolerate my unwillingness to open up. Thank you also for your unique ability to finally get me to do so. Thank you, Melinda, for your brilliant writing and for making Lava's story come to life on the preceding pages. To my agent, Julie Castiglia, thank you for believing in this project and for fighting to make this story a reality. You are a woman of passion and grace. Finally, thank you to my editor, Ann Treistman, who fell in love with the book and with Lava, and who has so magnificently turned our raw manuscript into a compelling read.

I hope you enjoyed Lava's tale and the journey he's taken. We thank you for reading his story and for your support of the young men and women in the uniforms of the US military.

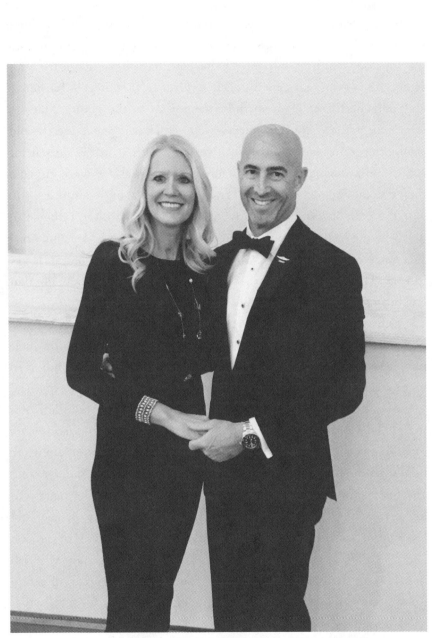

The author today attending a Marine Corps birthday ball with his girlfriend, Felena Hanson, founder of Hera Hub.